# Communicating
## *with the Public*

## A GUIDE FOR SCHOOL LEADERS

**Anne Meek**

*for Jim Pughsley
with all good
wishes,
Anne Meek*

Association for Supervision and Curriculum Development
Alexandria, Virginia USA

Association for Supervision and Curriculum Development
1703 N. Beauregard St. • Alexandria, VA 22311-1714 USA
Telephone: 1-800-933-2723 or 703-578-9600 • Fax: 703-575-5400
Web site: http://www.ascd.org • E-mail: member@ascd.org

Gene R. Carter, *Executive Director*
Michelle Terry, *Associate Executive Director, Program Development*
Nancy Modrak, *Director, Publishing*
John O'Neil, *Director of Acquisitions*
Julie Houtz, *Managing Editor of Books*
Carolyn R. Pool, *Associate Editor*
Kathleen Florio, *Copy Editor*

Charles D. Halverson, *Project Assistant*
Gary Bloom, *Director, Design and Production Services*
Karen Monaco, *Senior Designer*
Tracey A. Smith, *Production Manager*
Dina Murray, *Production Coordinator*
John Franklin, *Production Coordinator*
Valerie Sprague, *Desktop Publisher*
Winfield Swanson, *Indexer*

Printed in the United States of America.

August 1999 member book (p). ASCD Premium, Comprehensive, and Regular members periodically receive ASCD books as part of their membership benefits. No. FY99-9.

ASCD Stock No. 199052
ASCD member price: $18.95    nonmember price: $22.95

**Library of Congress Cataloging-in-Publication Data**
Meek, Anne.
    Communicating with the public : a guide for school leaders /
Anne Meek.
    p. cm.
  Includes index.
  ISBN 0-87120-343-X
  1. Schools—Public relations—United States. 2. Communication
in education—United States. I. Title.
  LB2847 .M43 1999
  659.2'9371—dc21
                                        99-6199
                                        CIP

04  03  02  01  00  99          10  9  8  7  6  5  4  3  2  1

# Communicating with the Public: A Guide for School Leaders

## List of Figures

*This book is dedicated to Beecher Clapp of Knoxville, Tennessee, my esteemed mentor and an influential leader in public education in Tennessee. In the course of developing a framework for the state curriculum in reading and language arts in the 1980s, it was Beecher who first sent me out for on-camera interviews with a TV news team. Beecher gave me a little nudge and a big smile and said, "Go on out there and talk to those reporters. You know what to say."*

# Acknowledgments

I wish to thank my husband, Gilbert L. Kraine, whose encouragement and forbearance over many months have made this book possible. I also thank Kerri Albertson and Steven Landfried, who reviewed the entire manuscript in draft and offered many helpful ideas about improving its usefulness, accuracy, and comprehensiveness.

In addition, I thank Joseph Lowenthal, who shared his excellent insights into the work of media liaisons and subsequently reviewed and improved Chapter 6; Patricia Terry and John Clement, whose suggestions about "How to Create a Home Page" (Appendix G) made that resource practical and timely; John McLaughlin for thoughtful suggestions about Chapter 5; and Carolyn Garrett for her assistance in improving Chapter 4.

I also wish to thank the editors at ASCD whose suggestions and skill greatly improved the book. Any deficiencies remaining are solely my responsibility.

# Preface: What This Book Is About

This book is about "baseline" communications in schools and school systems. Baseline communications are the ongoing efforts initiated by schools to meet the information needs of parents and the community at large, to strengthen the partnerships of parents and schools, to promote school activities and events, to explain school programs and school benefits, to enhance the image of the schools, and ultimately to promote support for education in the community.

The book is intended for K–12 educators in schools and central offices; it may also be useful to librarians, staff members from other nonprofit organizations, and postsecondary educators, all of whom will find the practical suggestions easy to adapt to those environments. Professors who teach community relations and the politics of education may find it helpful as a supplementary text.

In schools, there's an unwritten tradition that almost defines communication in terms of crises: a student is failing; asbestos contamination threatens a classroom; a group of parents is upset about the reading curriculum; a weather emergency looms on the horizon. Such crises leave us little choice but to *react*. In this book, you will find references to communicating during crises because, even in baseline efforts, crisis management is ever near. You'll also find specific resources for crisis management in the appendixes. But the main theme of this book is routine communications—the *proactive* efforts that address the information needs of school employees and the community and that seek long-term support for education.

Too often we have failed to recognize the potential of these baseline efforts. As a school principal, for example, I found my teachers apprehensive about parent conferences, a routine occurrence for communication. I wondered, *How could this be?* Teachers are socially skilled, adept at verbal communication, and knowledgeable about students and instructional programs. So how could they feel insecure? Part of the answer seemed to be the habit of waiting for a crisis, or at least for a problem, before we scheduled a conference. Naturally, if people don't talk until there's trouble, conflict is likely to occur, and anyone would be nervous just thinking about it.

But what if baseline communications are in place before problems arise? For example, suppose, at the beginning of the year, teachers send letters to parents giving information about their credentials and classroom expectations and inviting parents to visit. Suppose, when families enter the school, the office staff smiles and makes everyone feel at home. Suppose teachers learn conferencing techniques and begin to welcome the opportunity to talk with parents. These efforts build relationships with families and communities. They create the floor, the foundation, for all other efforts. Ultimately they build support for education.

Reaching out to parents and the community has come naturally throughout my career in education. As an early childhood teacher and again in middle schools, I always invited parents into the classroom to assist the children and me. As a principal, I established a parent volunteer program with the PTA, trained the teachers in conferencing techniques, and invited school board members to visit. I recruited community groups to develop a nature trail and build a play structure on the campus and to provide drama experiences, a week of "poetry in the school," performances

by the local symphony orchestra, and summer reading programs. As a supervisor, I worked with parents from many schools, participated in networking with civic organizations, and helped meet teachers' needs for information, face-to-face and in a newsletter. Later, after serving as managing editor of *Educational Leadership* for ASCD, I led communications efforts for a large city school system, creating print and video materials for external and internal audiences, working with the media, and providing executive services to the superintendent and the school board.

This book is my way of sharing with you part of what I've learned along the way. I hope it will help you to think deeply about school communications in general and, in particular, to design and organize a comprehensive communications program, created to reach your varied audiences and to teach them about your school or system, about all the marvelous activities taking place there, and about the caring, compassion, competence, and community in our schools today.

ANNE MEEK
Norfolk, Virginia
August 1999

# 1

# The Communications Imperative: Making Friends Before You Need Them

The best time to make friends is before you need them.
— Attributed to Lyndon B. Johnson

Only a few years ago, teachers and administrators could count on a fair amount of community support for schools—or at least on broad passive acceptance of their efforts. In those days, schools closely reflected the traditions and priorities of their local communities. In many communities, even when parents could afford the tuition for private or parochial education, public schools enrolled the majority of students. Indeed, in some areas, public schools were practically the only choice for most families. Whether private, public, or parochial schools were the choice, however, most families expected to stay put, the curriculum was relatively unchanging, and teachers typically taught for years, often in the same classroom. School affairs were predictable,

uneventful, even downright dull. Sometimes, wistfully, we call these "the good ol' days."

## The New School Environment

Today, schools operate in a demanding policy climate—one in which national, state, and local policymakers advocate new programs and curriculums, demand results, and scrutinize endless amounts of data to see whether schools are performing acceptably. The importance of schools in the economic development of both the nation and the local community, along with the potential of schools to contribute to the quality of life in a locality, has become increasingly clear. Education is also seen as overwhelmingly important to maintaining the preeminence of the United States in the global economy. In hometowns across the country, schools are seen as a major factor in economic development—the attraction of new businesses and the preservation of established businesses.

In addition, schools currently face a rather long list of expectations and needs generated by families, such as before- and after-school child care, along with the usual expectation for academics. Indeed, as clients, today's parents are demanding consumers—they know what they want, they have high standards for service, and they may complain loudly if they don't find services up to standard. Parents are accustomed to moving from place to place, often selecting housing based on the reputation of neighborhood schools. Thus, many families, especially middle-class families, choose where to send their children to school by selecting the neighborhood they prefer; others purchase private or parochial education. In addition, as voucher or choice provisions increase, many more parents may have the option of sending their children to schools outside their immediate neighborhoods.

Schools themselves have changed, too. Today's public schools possess a number of attributes and offer a variety of services and programs unheard of when today's parents were growing up—special education, programs for gifted and talented students, desegregation, interagency collaborations with social service agencies, and the like.

What's more, the curriculum is no longer the predictable entity it was in the past. New research findings and new concepts of how students learn, professional associations, religious conservatives, textbook and software publishers, as well as the demands of policymakers and business leaders contemplating the role of the United States in the global marketplace—all have influenced today's curriculum frameworks. What's more, today's schools serve *all* students, including those who might have, in an earlier era, quietly vanished from school to work on farms or in factories.

In short, profound changes have occurred in U.S. schools. School programs are different from those of the past. Parental needs and expectations have grown more complex and challenging. The environment in which schools operate—the policy climate—reflects an often critical attitude, with intense competition for tax dollars at a time when the majority of the public has no children in school.

Under such circumstances, educators face a new imperative: we must learn the basic principles of effective communications so as to inform, listen to, and learn from our various publics. As Lyndon Johnson said, we must "make friends before we need them."

## The Benefits of Proactive Communications

Today, when public support cannot be taken for granted, schools and school systems must find ways to build and strengthen connections with their communities. The foundation for strengthening connections and improving relationships is proactive communications. To establish baseline communications—to *reach* out to the community and then to *teach* about what is going on at school—promises great benefits in terms of moving toward ensuring optimum learning opportunities for students in school today and generating support for schools in the future.

## Strengthening Parent-School Partnerships

Sometime in the past, a popular parent-teacher covenant went like this: *I won't believe anything he says about you if you don't believe anything he says about me.* Seems quaint today, reflecting as it does suspicion of tales carried by children and implying that the adults in their lives need to establish direct communication with each other. Out of date, maybe, but the implied need is still timely. Communication is always the foundation of mutual respect, trust, and cooperation in relationships, and parent-teacher-student relationships are no exception. Schools that are proactive in communication will do the following:

• Increase mutual support between teachers and parents. Students understand that parents and teachers are working together, and this focuses students on behaving well and learning their lessons.

• Create "school-smart" parents. Well-informed parents are able to interpret school realities for their children (such as homework, grades, discipline, rules and requirements, and teamwork) and explain the benefits of education (such as college admissions, better jobs, and stature in the community).

• Create "home-smart" teachers. Well-informed teachers know the families of the children they teach as well as they know their subjects and can tailor their approaches to motivation and instruction accordingly.

## Meeting the Information Needs of Parents, Employees, and the Community at Large

With a baseline communications program in place, parents, school employees, and community members routinely receive more information about schools. Once school patrons learn they can depend on the school to disseminate accurate and timely information, community confidence in the professionalism of the school will increase. A comprehensive communications program will do the following:

• Increase awareness of basic school information, such as daily schedules, lunch menus, registration information, disciplinary procedures, bus schedules, PTA/PTSA/PTSO meetings and membership drives, and the like.

• Convey an attitude of openness and welcome on the part of the school.

• Demonstrate that the school or school system anticipates the information needs of its clientele, provides information without a hassle, and thus serves the public well.

• Create awareness that the school is well organized and knows its business.

• Inform employees, the public, and parents about where they can find specialized or additional information, such as where to go for help with problems, where to learn more about parenting, and how to assist the child with homework.

## Promoting School Activities and Events

The benefits of publicity for school activities and events are commonplace but important. Even when people simply read a news item in the local paper or see sound bites on TV, the publicity creates community awareness of what's going on in school. When more active patrons get the message, good communications will do the following:

• Increase attendance at athletic events, performances, meetings, awards ceremonies, and so forth.

• Increase box office, ticket, and concession revenues.

• Publicize student performances that are actually opportunities for exhibition and portfolio assessment by the community. These may include such events as play productions, athletic events including Special Olympics, and subject area competitions including art shows, musical performances, spelling bees, debates, and math contests.

• Build loyalty and allegiance to teams, choruses, bands, and other organizations; to students; and to the school as a whole.

• Bring more people into the schools, offering opportunities for recruiting volunteers, booster club members, sponsors of school-business partnerships, and others.

• Bring in people who do not have children in school but are interested in education and whose votes are important in school board elections, referendums, tax increases, and so forth.

• Develop community awareness of school needs, such as a new roof, parking spaces, athletic facilities, band uniforms, technology upgrades, and other resources and facilities.

• Publicize occasions when the public will informally scrutinize student behavior, thus strengthening community norms for student conduct.

## Explaining School Programs and School Benefits

Schools have become complex organizations, and no educator can safely assume that parents and citizens automatically know how schools work, what the role of the guidance counselor is, how students get medical care at school, what library/media specialists do on the job, and other similar specifics. A communications program that explains what's going on in schools will do the following:

• Generate increased awareness of and knowledge about new textbooks, technology use, curriculum frameworks, state mandates, and the like.

• Give parents background information about the curriculum that may enhance their ability to explain to their children the reasons for specific assignments and strategies.

- Help parents and the public to understand the changes in schools since they were students, including legal mandates, added services, and social influences.
- Create increased knowledge about whom to call with questions, thus personalizing the central administration and the school administration.
- Develop increased awareness of the benefits the schools provide at little or no cost: facilities for community use, sports and entertainment events, and workshops and presentations for various intellectual and parenting needs; scholarship searches; regulatory services for public health requirements such as vaccinations and physical examinations; and opportunities for volunteer service.

## Enhancing the Image of Schools

The image of an organization does not develop overnight, nor is it always created consciously. Unfortunately, the image of education has been tarnished because far too many schools and systems have been reluctant to communicate openly and broadly. Far too many communities have interpreted this reticence as evidence that schools have something to hide. Taking the initiative to communicate *begins* the process of image enhancement for schools. In the short run, proactive communications meet the information needs of the public. In the long run, a systematic and professional communications program creates a favorable image of your school or system. A comprehensive communications program will

do the following:

- Show that schools are open and responsive to their communities and have nothing to hide.
- Convey the impression that teachers and administrators know their business.
- Present individual and group accomplishments of students, teachers, and administrators.
- Collect community impressions, opinions, and issues for proactive responses.
- Establish and build trust and confidence in the school or school system.
- Recognize and strengthen community connections with the schools.

## Promoting Long-Term Support for Education

All of the benefits listed in this chapter begin to accrue almost as soon as schools take the initiative in communications. The hope for lasting support for education depends on the ongoing, cumulative effects of maintaining open and welcoming environments in the schools, continuing to provide responsive and competent professional services to the community, and always valuing and strengthening relationships with employees, citizens, parents, and the students themselves.

# Taking the Initiative in Communications: Another Kind of Teaching

When it comes to communications, silence is not golden. Educators must demonstrate the benefits of schools and schooling, build and maintain trust and confidence in their work within their communities, and strengthen the partnership of teachers and parents on behalf of students. It is not enough to educate children in their hometowns or across the nation without telling the world about the whole process. Educators must open their hearts and minds, their schoolhouse doors, and their lines of communication to teach their communities about schools.

Educators are often shy about taking the initiative in communications. This reluctance is genuine. It stems from a real desire to make the world a better place. In their hearts and minds, promoting themselves is unworthy and ignoble; they are self-effacing. But reaching out to others to explain schools is not self-promotion—it's another kind of teaching. In their classrooms, educators determine the

messages they want their students to get—that's the curriculum. And the way they shape the messages for students at various ages and stages—that's instruction.

Let me give an example. The K–12 language arts curriculum is one long series of messages of academic content to impart to students. Teachers shape the messages to suit the ages, levels of prior knowledge, learning styles, and interests and abilities of the many students who must receive them. In other words, teachers adjust the messages to fit the audience that is expected to receive them. This is second nature to educators.

Communicating with various audiences is only an expansion of teachers' roles. When teaching responsibilities are extended to include the entire community, educators can feel comfortable with taking the initiative in communications.

# 2

# Planning to Communicate

Honest information has always been the lifeblood of democracy.
—THOMAS KUNKEL*

The purpose of this book is to promote proactive communications, the ongoing day-to-day communications that should form the baseline for every school and system. So often, educators must communicate during a crisis—*reacting* to a lost child, a student brawl, the arrest of a staff member, or community unrest about a new textbook. But to gain the benefits of baseline communications, educators must become *proactive*.

To start taking the initiative, you can begin by predicting the events and activities of the school year in order to anticipate the information needs of your school community. You can then think about what you need to say in terms of what each segment of the community wants or needs to know. Then you can identify the means—or the vehicles—for conveying your messages to the varied audiences, and determine your major goals and strategies for reaching those varied audiences. In other words, to be proactive, you must *plan* to communicate—just as if you were planning to teach lessons to different groups of students, as discussed in Chapter 1.

The advantage of a plan is that it gives you a big-picture way of looking at communications functions. A plan helps you to know you're covering all the bases and gives you a frame of reference for checking your own work. What's more, the process of developing a plan can be the basis for seeking ideas from your faculty, your PTA/PTSA/PTSO, and other groups in your community, too. Feedback from others will help to improve your plan; at the same

---

*Kunkel, T. (1998, August 30). The pen is mightier than the six-shooter. *New York Times Book Review, Sec. 7*, p. 25.

7

time your effort to seek suggestions helps to create a sense of openness and professionalism.

## Starting Where You Are

A communications plan has several major elements:

- Goals—The important ongoing functions you want to emphasize or the immediate priorities identified for a specified time period.
- Strategies—The means by which you hope to achieve your goals.
- Vehicles—The ways the strategies come alive.
- Audiences—The varied groups within your community and within your school or system.
- Messages—The varied information that you need to send out or that the different audiences desire.
- Evaluation—The methods by which you measure what your plan accomplishes.

Communications plans may also include additional elements, such as an extended breakdown of the tasks and subtasks necessary for accomplishing the strategies; the names of persons responsible for each task; and the specific target dates for the completion of each. What's described here is a simplified approach, which assumes you can include any necessary additional elements.

The preceding list implies that the planning process is linear, but it may not be. You may be doing many other things while you are trying to write your plan, and you may not have the time to quickly develop an elaborate document with all the elements in place. In that case, you may find it helpful to start by listing the various groups who should be hearing from the school, to see whether you are reaching everyone you need to reach. Or you may start with a successful example, such as a good newsletter, and see how you can expand on that by putting it on a home page. You should feel perfectly comfortable with letting the details of your plan evolve over time, while you use the major elements listed above to check out the big picture in communications at your school or in your system. What's important is to keep in mind the overall concepts while you work out the details. In other words, start where you are.

A word of caution here. Overall or general systemwide strategic plans, currently so popular in organizations, are often quite limited in their scope. Remember that the rationale for developing them is to set *priorities* within the system. But a focus on priorities may obscure the *ongoing functions* that are still expected even when overlooked or taken for granted in planning. These ongoing functions may in fact actually be *the continuous daily activities that achieve the mission of the school system*.

Suppose, for example, the overall strategic plan for a large system sets forth goals for (1) a reading initiative, (2) upgrading technology and training, (3) providing early childhood education for at-risk preschoolers, and (4) improving test scores. These are, for the duration of the plan, the priorities for the system. These priorities, however, do not directly address continuous efforts—such as the development of a superior teaching force, the coordination and support necessary to achieve excellence in instruction in all grades and subjects, or baseline communications.

First, if your system or school already has an overall strategic plan in place, you can check that plan to see whether it includes communications objectives or strategies. If they are, take a close look at them. Are they limited to the priorities expressed by the goals? Or do they include the ongoing functions? Do they include everything you need to get across in baseline communications? If necessary, perhaps you can expand the existing objectives or strategies so that communications are included. Second, if you find the existing plan includes no communications goals or strategies, you can propose revising the plan to include communications. Third, if your system is just beginning the process of overall strategic planning, you can point out that now's the time to ensure that the planning team includes communications goals or strategies.

On the other hand, if your school or system does not have an existing plan, the task of developing a communications plan is not difficult. The sample goals and plans in this book address both immediate priorities and ongoing, continuous functions. In general, the goals address ongoing functions, and the strategies address priorities. The strategies are designed to be updated annually, to stay current and

address immediate needs. Just remember: Whatever approach you take, planning enables you to proactively address all aspects of communications—and that's what's important.

## Two Sample Communications Goals

To illustrate how such goals and accompanying strategies may look, here are sample goals from two plans. The audience for each goal is listed, along with vehicles for each strategy. A brief discussion follows each strategy. (The complete plans—"A Sample School Communications Plan" and "A Sample Systemwide Communications Plan"—appear in Appendixes A and B.)

### A School Goal

*Goal:* Provide information about student progress, student learning and achievement, and school programs, events, and activities.

*Audience:* Parents, caregivers, and families; citizens and the public.

*Strategy 1:* Provide welcome packets for new families whenever new students enroll and to all families at the beginning of each school year; include school calendar, grading policies, discipline procedures, school rules, guidance services, emergency communications plan, bus schedule and routes, staff lists, and so on.

a. Select and order school folders in school colors with logo, school name and address.

b. Develop or collect all pertinent documents; duplicate; maintain files in office.

c. Prepare packets as needed for new families; store in office cabinet for easy access.

d. Distribute as new students enroll; coordinate with student welcome packets.

*Vehicle:* Routine information packaged in school folders, with letter welcoming patrons.

> *Discussion:* School folders, created especially for holding the many documents that explain the day-to-day experiences children will have in school, provide a good way to organize information for easy use, and they create positive feelings toward the school. An elementary school we know relies on PTA funding for the folders, and the school sustains the costs of preparing and photocopying all other material.

*Strategy 2:* Send all families weekly newsletters with up-to-date meeting notices, class news and activities, menus, and parenting tips.

a. Purchase yearlong supply of bright yellow paper (the "color of the year") for newsletters.

b. Collect pertinent information from faculty and staff at staff meetings or through a form.

c. Get copy typed into newsletter format; proofread, duplicate, and distribute.

d. Announce schedule for distribution and "color of the year" at first PTA meeting.

*Vehicle:* School newsletters.

> *Discussion:* An elementary principal learned early in her career that many newsletters suffer from "book bag death," never reaching the parents until it's too late. Now she uses neon colors for her school newsletters and announces at the first PTA meeting the "color of the year," alerting parents to look for that color among the children's papers. Neon colors stand out even inside a book bag!

*Strategy 3:* Provide program brochures about each faculty and staff member, explaining their programs and credentials.

a. Discuss concept at staff meeting and request pertinent information from each staff member.

b. Appoint staff committee to oversee the collection of information and production of brochures.

c. Review and approve all brochures before duplication and distribution.

d. Locate and set up info-file in hallway near office.

*Vehicles:* One-page desktop-designed brochures; info-file.

> *Discussion:* That same principal, with the assistance of a faculty member who did the desktop design, developed individual brochures with a simple, standard design. She began with brochures for each classroom and expanded to brochures for library, guidance, office, cafeteria, and custodial staff. Written in a friendly, down-to-earth tone, these brochures let

parents know the basics about each classroom and each support service. Available from the hallway info-file, the brochures created a sense of professionalism for the faculty and staff.

*Strategy 4:* Improve conferencing techniques; schedule conferences at convenient times to suit individual parent schedules; include students in conferences as appropriate.

*Vehicles:* Training sessions; conference days.

*Discussion:* Face-to-face communication deserves attention, too. Another principal found that communications at her school were above average except in conferencing techniques. She provided training in active listening, along with a plan for the stages in a conference. The stages included a later checkpoint, so that parents and teachers alike could check on the effectiveness of the improvement strategies decided upon during the conference. Teachers found that conferences became more productive and less stressful; parents felt their input was taken seriously and they had a way to be sure the plans for the student were being followed [see Appendix H, "How to Conduct Effective Parent-Teacher(-Student) Conferences"].

*Strategy 5:* Expand into electronic communications. Determine feasibility of a homework hot line or voice messaging system and install, if possible; select software, develop procedures, and design and implement school home page.

*Vehicles:* In-school planning and budgeting processes.

*Discussion:* Planning for a voice messaging system, a homework hot line, or a home page is important, because each requires funding and technical support. Schools that use voice messaging systems to phone parents about PTA meetings find that attendance goes up; homework hot lines receive numerous calls per week. A home page may be created by a teacher or parent who has the technical capacity to create one, and software is now available to make the move from print to electronics (see Appendix G, "How to Create a Home Page").

## A Systemwide Goal

The central office perspective requires a host of different functions addressing the variety of schools and services in the entire school system. Also, central office concerns focus on the overall image of the system in the larger community and the policy and practice concerns of the superintendent and the school board.

*Goal:* Raise public and employee awareness of systemwide events, programs, services, and goals.

*Audience:* Employees, parents and families, the media, and the general public.

*Strategy 1:* Develop and maintain procedures for routine communications functions.

a. Create working calendar of events for interoffice use on paper and online.

b. Establish a master production calendar that includes all publications and TV shows.

c. Update lists of media contacts four times yearly; distribute.

d. Provide staff development sessions for all administrators and media liaisons: four sessions for administrators (one required, three voluntary) and two sessions for media liaisons (required). Update their information about policies, procedures, changes, and so forth.

*Vehicles:* Calendar of events; production calendar; lists of media contacts, with special assignments noted (crises, public affairs, features, etc.); training sessions.

> *Discussion:* Achieving such a large and ongoing goal day after day requires many supporting details. Listing the tactics under Strategy 1 helps to focus your attention on the smaller tasks that keep routine communications moving smoothly. Also important is the recurring need to update the training of the other people who share responsibility for communications.

*Strategy 2:* Update and distribute procedures for emergency or crisis situations.

a. On list of media contacts, indicate those with specific emergency responsibilities.

b. Maintain/update list of procedures for specific emergency situations.

c. Maintain file of disaster drills for each school and every other facility.

d. Maintain contact with emergency management offices and city departments and up-to-date list of locations of hazardous sites; maintain files of action plans for emergency management.

e. Develop sample school handbook for assistance with emergencies at schools; distribute to principals for review and feedback; budget funds for production and for staff development in next school year.

*Vehicles:* Lists of media contacts with special assignments noted (crises, public affairs, features, etc.); procedures for specific emergency situations; disaster drills; files for materials from emergency management offices; draft school handbook for review.

> *Discussion:* Just as it's important to update the routine logistical information for Strategy 1, it's important to keep emergency or crisis management current. Be on the alert for policy changes that also influence crisis management—school safety is always a hot topic. Networking with local, state, and federal contacts will

help you in this regard. The dissemination of information about procedures, along with the accompanying training, is valuable to both internal audiences (school employees) and external audiences (parents and the community).

**Strategy 3:** Coordinate centralized efforts with school-based information strategies.

a. Exchange information daily or as needed among superintendent's office, all principals, legislative liaison, staff in community relations, and staff in pupil personnel management. Improve reliability of incident-reporting process.

b. Present delineation of school-based and centralized functions to media liaisons during training sessions; seek feedback; improve understanding of who does what.

c. Provide staff development on school board policies related to media and community relations, orientation to the communications program, and an overview of the services and functions provided by the staff.

**Vehicles:** Phone calls; charts; staff development.

> **Discussion:** Strategy 3 is not exactly obvious, until you think about the importance of avoiding turf battles in projecting the image of the school system. When school efforts are coordinated with central office efforts, the news media have an easier time getting the

news they need for the larger community and thus perceive that school employees are expert at their duties. At the same time, school employees can deal with good news or bad news in a confident manner when they know the lines of communication across the entire organization. As usual, staff development about these expectations is necessary to ensure understanding.

**Strategy 4:** Support initiatives of the superintendent and the school board.

a. Assist with superintendent's correspondence, both routine and specialized; maintain computer files of sample letters; develop binder and diskette of form letters.

b. Prepare superintendent's speeches; deliver in presentation binders with supporting information about the event: place, time, day, organization, name of contact on site, other honored guests and community leaders likely to attend.

c. Prepare op-ed pieces for the local newspaper to explain initiatives and support marketing campaigns.

d. Publicize board meetings, issues under consideration, and subsequent actions.

e. Organize specific marketing campaigns regarding technology use in schools and capital and operating budget needs.

**Vehicles:** Form letters in binder and on diskette; local newspapers and employee and parent newsletters; local media outlets.

*Discussion:* At the central office, providing support for upper-level decision makers is a major emphasis, as this strategy illustrates. As shown here, one way to help manage the heavy volume of the superintendent's correspondence is to develop form letters for a mail-merge system, even though individually written letters will be needed occasionally. Requests for speeches will vary according to occasions and invitations, and the need for op-ed pieces will vary according to issues; but both kinds of requests are likely to be made often.

When the superintendent and school board select major initiatives for implementation, such as increased funding for technology or curriculum standards and new assessments, planning for the marketing campaign to inform the public and parents demands much attention, and routine announcements about meetings, issues, and actions are needed continuously. For example, while conducting a campaign to raise parent and community awareness about the uses of technology in schools, a central administrator in a large system developed a detailed campaign plan that incorporated school open houses to showcase the uses of technology; news stories in local media outlets, including cable TV shows; articles in systemwide parent and employee newsletters and in individual school newsletters; and repeated news releases from both the central office and individual schools. The written plan was presented to the school board as an information item.

*Strategy 5:* Identify newsworthy events and programs, and prepare media campaigns to support or publicize them.

a. Coordinate editorial needs of media contacts with school system efforts.

b. Collaborate with colleagues to showcase accomplishments.

*Vehicles:* Local media outlets; systemwide parent and employee newsletters; TV shows.

*Discussion:* No matter what the size of the system, there are always events and activities worthy of media coverage. These may include science fairs, exemplary instructional programs, athletic championships, school recognitions such as accreditation by an outside agency or designation as a "blue-ribbon school," and the like. Colleagues across the system can contact the communications staff whenever good news happens, and the staff will employ the usual tactics of preparing news releases, making media calls, and promoting the spread of the good news via school and system newsletters, cable TV shows, and home pages.

∽ ∽ ∽

Without planning, you are not teaching your own lessons as proactively as possible. You are letting the news media choose the messages the public receives. It's not possible for you to change the news media, but you can influence them. You can flood them with accurate and excellent information about schools. You *can* reach your own audiences and teach your own lessons.

# 3

# Shaping Your Messages for Your Audiences

People are down on what they ain't up on.

—WILL ROGERS

In putting your communications plan into action, it's helpful to think of the goals in terms of the messages you need to get across—the many and varied messages from your school or system throughout the year. For example, for a global goal such as "Provide information about student progress, student learning and achievement, and school programs, events, and activities," what messages are implied? If you are to be proactive, what is it that you want or need to tell people?

Off the top of your head, you might reply:

Oh, we want people to know the school is safe, we welcome students, and we have a stimulating program—and oh, yes, this is an accredited school. We want parents to visit the school and come to us when they have a problem.

We should explain our reading program, and we should be sure to have the lunch schedule handy— all the schedules, especially sports. There are lots of meetings to publicize, too. And, personally, I'd like to tell the whole community about those events, too, so they'll support us when we need that new classroom addition. . . .

Exactly right! There are many messages to get out. But even in close-knit communities, not every person needs or wants to know the same message at the same time. Not every person gets information from the same vehicles or cares about school messages to start with. How can you determine which messages go to which audience segments or which groups are interested in which information?

16

For the sake of familiarity, let's return to the teaching analogy. The message you want to send—that's the curriculum. The way you tailor or shape the message to suit the varied audiences in your community—that's instruction. When teaching, teachers don't present curriculum content to all students in the same way. They select and present content based on the needs, interests, and abilities of the learners, but always adhering to the dictates of the curriculum. (Sure, as teachers, they can "wing it" when an unexpected teachable moment occurs—say, when monarch butterflies make a sudden stop at the playground on their autumnal migration; that kind of exception merely proves teachers can adapt to the interests of the students). Their professional expertise lies in shaping the curriculum message to the characteristics of the particular classes, or audiences, they are teaching.

Later in this chapter you'll find a discussion about the advantages of using plain language, not jargon, in all your communications efforts. The advantages are not limited to any one audience segment but apply to all.

Before you can determine the vehicles for getting all the messages out, it's a good idea to analyze your audience, just as you would diagnose learning styles, developmental levels, and special needs and abilities if you were in the classroom. To start with, think of the external audience—those outside the school or system—and the internal audience—those inside the school or system. Under those two categories, list the major groups. Add subgroups if there are any—and there certainly are in the "parents" group. This analysis puts you well on your way toward understanding which messages should go to which audience. You'll also find it easy to shape your messages according to the interests and perspectives of the groups.

## The External Audiences

The external audiences for school communications are quite broad, encompassing major groups within the community. Identifying the needs and interests of each audience segment is mostly a matter of common sense. The following discussion starts with perhaps the most familiar group addressed by schools—parents—and continues with other segments that may be easily overlooked.

### Parents and Caregivers: A Variety of Family Constellations

Parents, other caregivers, and families in general have many information needs in common. They will need registration information, course and curriculum descriptions, bus schedules, lunch schedules, information about student activities, report card schedules, testing schedules, parent and student handbooks, the annual school calendar, and the like. Remember that family units have widely varied characteristics. Single-parent families are common. Grandparents and other relatives often have major responsibilities for bringing up children. In addition, many students live in foster homes and agency-sponsored group homes. In shaping messages for such a variety of family constellations, try to avoid stereotypes; don't describe the audience for your newsletter as "mom and dad," for example, but as "families of students." Be aware of the differing languages used in your school community, and provide newsletters and bulletins in as many languages as possible.

Within the overall group, it's easy to see subgroups. For example, parents of students with disabilities have particular needs for information, as do parents of children in gifted and talented programs. Typically, information needs also differ among the families of students in various grade levels or programs. For example, parents of entering kindergartners must be informed about immunization and physical exam requirements, readiness tests, and the philosophy and methods of early childhood education. In middle school and high school, information about course offerings, extracurricular activities, athletic teams, vocational programs, alternative schools, and graduation requirements becomes important, as well as information about preparation for college admissions and the job market.

Beyond the more or less logistical stuff such as bus routes and menus, parents are interested in policy decisions, instructional methods, curriculum content, textbook selection, teacher qualifications, safety and discipline topics, and school-based services such as child care. As busy as they are, most families have a lively interest in what's going on in the schools. They are savvy about the influence of school programs and environments on their children,

likely to be demanding and even critical, and likely to expect to exert maximum influence on those programs and environments.

Information about student learning and achievement is, perhaps, the biggest challenge. Report cards and interim progress reports, as important as they are, are just the beginning. You can keep parents informed by sending home graded papers or student work folders, homework assignments, and "happy notes" for accomplishments, or by making phone calls when necessary. For homework assignments, many schools now are implementing "homework hot lines" or voice messaging systems, and these are an excellent choice when you can fund and support them. Conferences offer great potential for two-way communication, giving parents and teachers (and students, too) the chance to talk over the student's interests, study habits, attitudes toward different subjects, potential for improvement, and many other specific topics. [For tips on "How to Conduct Effective Parent-Teacher(-Student) Conferences," see Appendix H.]

Most schools offer support and assistance for helping students succeed in school and for helping parents improve their parenting skills. Parenting workshops; conferences with teachers, guidance counselors, and principals; college nights, with program and scholarship information; explanations of the curriculum; and programs that focus on "family math" or reading aloud to children—you can make all sorts of sessions available, according to the needs of your school or community. It is wise to assess the needs of those attending for translations into other languages, including sign language.

In addition to the presentation of information and the demonstration of skills, such meetings offer abundant opportunities for face-to-face communication with parents and families. Face-to-face communication enables people to ask the questions of most importance to them and to receive answers from the school presenters. In other words, it's two-way communication and therefore highly desirable. Hearing parent concerns is important, as is finding the answers to their specific questions, because parent concerns may represent issues of wide interest in the community and therefore merit the attention of the administration. Emerging parent concerns may also indicate directions for the school or system to consider seriously, such as unmet needs in materials or services, unhealthy conditions in buildings or on playing fields, or confusion about the implementation of state standards or testing programs. (See the box "Tips for Communicating with Parents and Caregivers.")

## Opinion Leaders:
## Politically Savvy, Active, and Sensitive

Opinion leaders, often called key communicators, are the people who get things done in any community. They include elected and appointed officials; leaders in parent associations and advisory groups; officers and activists from civic clubs, homeowners associations, and ethnic groups; leaders of all kinds of community organizations; religious leaders; advocates for various causes; and the

---

### ∞ T I P S ∞
### For Communicating with
### Parents and Caregivers

• Identify the information needs of families in general, and then determine the varying information needs of different groups according to grade levels, regular education, special education, gifted and talented programs, languages spoken at home, and so forth.

• Look beyond these basic needs, and help families find the next level of information when they want it—information such as school board actions, curriculum implementation, textbook selection, and school volunteer opportunities.

• Remember, too, that parents and caregivers are usually interested in parenting workshops and presentations on helping their children be successful in school or on preparing for college and the job market; and in information on before- and after-school child care, intramural sports, and clubs.

• Be sensitive to the many family patterns in the world today, and avoid stereotyping people and cultural groups.

sometimes invisible but always influential behind-the-scenes leaders. Their support is critical to the success of public schools. Keep in mind that they may need newsletters in languages other than English. Their information needs are likely to focus on policy issues, the direction and mission of the schools, impending decisions, and economic and civic matters. In other words, they are interested in actions of the school board, the quality of life in the community, and fair treatment of their constituents.

Opinion leaders are likely to be politically savvy, politically active, and politically sensitive. And they *are* key communicators; so when they have accurate and positive information about schools to pass on, that's what they'll pass on. If their information about schools is inaccurate or negative, unfortunately, that's what they will have to disseminate. (See the box "Tips for Communicating with Opinion Leaders.")

## Economic Development Offices and Chambers of Commerce: Selling Quality of Life

In today's economy, state and local governments, as well as chambers of commerce, are usually involved in economic development efforts for their communities. The clients and staffs of these offices are an important audience for school information, because good schools are a major quality-of-life factor in attracting businesses to the community. Their information needs are likely to run the gamut, depending upon requests from company officials and employees.

First of all, this audience likes material that gives a general overview of the school system—its programs and services; an annual report format is ideal for this purpose. But the official staff also will forward specific requests to the schools for detailed information on such topics as registration, the curriculum, services for students with disabilities, the school calendar, and the like. It is wise also to be alert to any school requirements specific to your state or community if companies considering relocation from another locale will be bringing

---

∞ **TIPS** ∞
**For Communicating with Opinion Leaders**

- Develop a contact list of opinion leaders, and update it as often as needed to stay current. It should include each person's name, organization, office held, address, phone number, fax number, and e-mail address.
- Invite these important constituents to selected school events, programs, and activities.
- Send school newsletters to opinion leaders, just as you do to parents and families.
- Send copies of news releases to opinion leaders or to their staffs or to other officers of their organizations.

employees to your town. For example, if your state has a "gateway" test at a certain grade level or performance standards that must be met at several grade levels, newcomers who will be enrolling their children in the schools need this information. (See the box "Tips for Communicating with Economic Development Offices and Chambers of Commerce.")

## Retired People and Seniors: Concerned About Schools and Taxes

Retired people in your community (who may or may not be seniors or "golden-agers") constitute an audience segment you must not overlook, even if you don't see them often. They rarely have children in the schools but are a major portion of the tax base. As a group, they may be wary of tax expenditures and alarmed about young people today. Yet they are among the strongest supporters of schools. They want good schools, respectful students, and qualified teachers, along with low taxes. Too often, their information needs are overlooked by educators. They need reassurance that schools are orderly, that students are learning the basics, that teachers are actively teaching, and that their tax dollars are well spent. They will not be impressed with trends and fads, new teaching methods, or what they may regard as "window dressing," such as programs to improve self-esteem.

Rather, retired people and seniors respond well to information about how teachers are instilling good manners, good study habits, and academic content in their students, along with

a great deal of self-sufficiency and self-respect. They need information that explains clearly that the curriculum does, indeed, teach students to spell, to use an index, to calculate without a calculator, and so forth. Retired people do not usually relate well to the jargon of education trends, and they shouldn't have to. Just explain school news in a positive tone and in jargon-free language that reassures them

### ∞ TIPS ∞
### For Communicating with Economic Development Offices and Chambers of Commerce

• Establish a working relationship with your local economic development office and chamber of commerce so as to determine specific needs identified by the corporate and businesspeople who are thinking of relocating to your community. Identify a contact person within the office.

• Include the contact person on mailing lists for school and systemwide newsletters.

• Respond to requests promptly. Requests are likely to vary from the need for general overviews when these groups are recruiting businesses to highly individual and personal needs once a business is seriously considering relocation to your community.

about the eternal verities in teaching and learning—basic skills, homework, preparation for tests, and good performance on tests and on applying knowledge to practical problems. Then you'll communicate effectively with this group.

Retired people are often news junkies; they can be reached through local newspapers and TV as well as community cable channels and city or county publications. It's also a good idea to provide regular columns about school news to the newsletter editors of chapters of the American Association of Retired Persons (AARP), civic leagues, and churches. You may be able to adapt news items originally written for parent and employee newsletters for this purpose, to keep the service manageable in terms of your own time. Or organizations may be able to adapt your regularly issued news releases for their newsletters. You can easily add the names of contact persons, along with their fax numbers, to your distribution list for news releases.

Just like any other audience segment, older people value face-to-face communications, such as speakers at their club meetings who can answer specific questions with reliable information and a reassuring manner. Just remember that face-to-face communication, with its high number of nonverbal cues, gives words deeper and richer meaning. Seniors and retired people also have their own individual concerns; their questions are not always easy to classify. Face-to-face interactions enable you to address individual questions adequately, even if you have

to call someone back with an answer. And you can listen and learn, and inform the principal or superintendent about their concerns.

Seniors and retired people usually benefit from—and enjoy—classroom and school visitations, with time afterward to ask questions about what they saw. In addition, schools strengthen positive connections through intergenerational tutoring, grandparents' days, and student visits to retirement homes and civic groups, complete with chorus or combo performances and favors such as student artwork or letters. An effective strategy from a high school we know, for example, is to offer "senior passports" to retired people—free tickets to school events.

Seniors and retired people make excellent volunteers, and PTAs/PTOs/PTSAs often recruit them to donate time and expertise to schools. The opportunity to interact with youngsters can be an attraction for seniors separated by long distances from their biological children and grandchildren. For example, one large suburban elementary school in a highly mobile community held "Adopt-a-Grandparent Day" for seniors who didn't see enough of their own grandchildren and then recruited volunteers from among the guests. In a small rural school, to enrich their study of the early history of the nation, students invited seniors from the neighborhood to tell stories about the original land grants and early settlements. In addition to enrichment activities, tutoring, and mentoring, seniors and retirees often can provide technical services to schools, for example, installing computers and software or creating home pages. The volunteer services can be one-time or ongoing.

Never underestimate the power of interacting with students to maintain the support of older people for the schools. People who feel they are truly making a difference in students' lives are often willing to give additional time and to increase their support for schools. Appreciation is a great reward for retired people and seniors who donate their time to schools and students. Try not to run out of tokens of appreciation, and remember that statements of gratitude and cards and letters from the students themselves are always welcome. (See the box "Tips for Communicating with Retired People and Seniors.")

## The Media: Real People with a Job to Do

Media representatives—reporters, editors, and camera crews—serve as a channel for getting news and information to the community at large. As such, they are a very important audience for anyone who wants to strengthen support for schools. You can build good relationships with them by taking their needs seriously and helping them to do their jobs effectively. There will always be some tension between your desire to protect your school and their desire to tell the news, but to concentrate on the adversarial nature of the relationship is shortsighted. Educators need to make friends with media representatives in order to ensure positive coverage or, at the least, fair treatment of school news.

### ∞ TIPS ∞
### For Communicating with Retired People and Seniors

• Cultivate face-to-face communications wherever and whenever possible, and realize that many seniors and retired people are news junkies, absorbing news from daily TV news shows, talk radio, local newspapers, and specialty tabloids.

• Emphasize, in publications and news, good discipline, basic skills, active teaching, and the return on tax dollars.

• Avoid jargon and trends and fads; use plain English and relate information to the "eternal verities" of teaching and learning.

• Send school news items and regularly issued news releases to appropriate organizations for use in their newsletters.

• Collaborate with parent associations to recruit retired people and seniors as volunteer tutors and mentors.

• Capitalize on their need to have contact with children and young people, especially among those who are grandparents and are not geographically close to their biological children and grandchildren.

• Show abundant appreciation for all they do for your students and your school.

First, reporters and editors must have prompt attention to their requests. In the news business, tight deadlines are the name of the game. When faced with a request, always ask "What's your deadline?" Then indicate when you'll call back with the requested information. The matter of tight deadlines can be a problem if you are dependent upon the assistance of others in the school to meet a deadline. In the immediate situation, you may need to promise later assistance to a colleague, as a trade-off, in order to free up the time for that colleague to get the information you need before the deadline.

In the long run, it's worth the effort to familiarize school employees with the way the news business works and to create empathy for the pressures faced by reporters and editors. For example, a regular meeting of teachers or administrators can include a briefing from a reporter or an assignment editor on the functions and frustrations of deadlines. Further, you can point out the benefits of good relationships with the media, then explain that timely responses are necessary for maintaining those good relationships—and, therefore, for maintaining the positive image of the school or the system. With persuasion and patience, you may improve your response time to media requests overall. (For brief guidelines suitable for distribution at meetings, consult Appendix I, "Media Relations at a Glance.")

Sometimes deadlines are relaxed. For example, a reporter may be working on a story that is not intended for tomorrow's headlines or the evening news, but is to be used when other

news doesn't crowd it out. In general, these are features and human interest stories, not hard news, and they are usually favorable to the school and system. But you still need to know what the time frame is, so that you can respond promptly to the reporter. It is your job to meet their schedules, not their job to meet yours.

Another service to media reporters and editors is that of filling requests made under the various state Freedom of Information acts. These state laws usually mirror the provisions of the 1966 federal Freedom of Information Act but pertain to state jurisdictions. Such requests are usually filed in search of information needed for hard news stories, often regarding sensitive topics; and the time frames for a response are spelled out in the law. Consult the office of the attorney general in your state or your own school system's legal counsel for the specifics of the law in your state. There are some exemptions to the disclosure requirements. In your role, it would be helpful to become familiar with the time frames, the exemptions, and the types of records or information you are required to provide.

An important criterion for service to media representatives is accuracy. It may be time-consuming to track down the details needed to answer a question or to find the supporting documents that will flesh out a story, but it's worth it. No one's needs are well served by misleading or inaccurate information. When there are questions that cannot be answered because of policy or administrative direction, you can explain straightforwardly that no information can be released on that topic and state the reasons in general terms, such as "Confidentiality is required," "This is a personnel matter," or "No action has been taken at this time."

Working with the news media sometimes involves the phenomenon of fast-breaking news, which means there will be changes in the known "facts" from moment to moment. In covering a school fire, for example, the damage estimate may change from day to day, as new information comes to light about the extent of the fire, the nature of structural damage, the presence of asbestos, and the destruction of textbooks and personal collections of instructional materials. Experience suggests you should qualify your pronouncements on any given day. For example, you can say "Preliminary estimates . . ." or "Rough estimates indicate . . . but the engineers have not completed their assessment of the structural damage, and we expect better figures late this week." In this way, you will acknowledge the changing nature of what is known as the crisis unfolds, and that will help to ensure your credibility. (See sources dealing with crisis management in Appendix J.)

These situations will inevitably include instances in which the next day brings new information to light, changing the facts of the day before. Therefore, in the midst of fast-breaking news, it is wise to develop a few stock phrases in advance, so that your quotations can meet the immediate needs of reporters and also maintain accuracy about where officials are in the ongoing process of figuring out the ramifications of the crisis. Incidentally, no apologies

are necessary when the information changes from day to day—that's what the news business is all about—but explanations of this phenomenon can help your colleagues to understand the nature of the news.

Occasionally, if you explain a seemingly negative situation with facts and perspectives, you may succeed in "killing" a hostile story. For example, a TV talk show host in a large city received a tip from an irate citizen who had seen school system cars parked at a fine resort hundreds of miles from town on a Saturday. The central office staffer tracked down the employees involved and then candidly explained to the talk show host that the occasion was a professional meeting and that the employees who stayed over an extra day were paying their own expenses. The talk show host, receiving this explanation, did not pursue the story further. In another situation, an upset parent had phoned a local newspaper reporter, indignant over the closing of school in inclement weather. The reporter inquired why the decision had been made in a way that caused such inconvenience to families. When a staffer explained the elaborate decision making necessary on such occasions—consultations with nearby school superintendents, transportation officials, observers across the area, and the weather service, as well as considerations of time of day, parents' work schedules, liability implications, and the like—the reporter declined to write the critical story she had had in mind when she heard the parent's complaint. In fact, she dropped the topic entirely.

In both these cases, factual explanations persuaded the reporters that negative stories were not warranted and would indeed have been a disservice to readers and viewers, as well as to the school system.

The media outlets in your community are a key source of information for *all* audience segments. The news may reach your entire community only in fragments and rarely in a comprehensive way; still, media outlets are a conduit to the audiences you want to reach. Thus, they remain overwhelmingly important in getting your messages out. They deserve all the respect and attention you can give them. (See the box "Tips for Communicating with the Media.")

---

### ∞ T I P S ∞
### For Communicating with the Media

• Think of media representatives as a separate audience of real people, and cultivate friendly relationships with reporters, editors, and camera crews at all times. Remember, "They have more ink than you do."

• Recognize that news releases are your main vehicle for reaching media representatives, and tailor them to meet the needs of reporters and editors. Give advance notice of all events, and fax news releases routinely. Make follow-up phone calls when you want coverage for a particular story about your school. (For specific guidelines, see Appendix C, "How to Write a News Release.")

• Develop the habit of asking "What's your deadline?" whenever a reporter or an editor asks you for information or an interview. Deadlines are a fact of life in their line of work and must be respected if you desire the benefits of good working relationships.

• Learn how to deal with fast-breaking news, in which the "facts" change overnight. Prepare sensible phrases in advance to use in quotations, phrases that will convey the changing nature of what is known from day to day.

• Become familiar with the requirements of your state's Freedom of Information Act.

• Always thank a reporter or an editor for fair treatment, even if the story delivers bad news. For positive treatment, send thank-you letters from students as well as your own letter. If your school is treated unfairly or incorrectly, send a note to the reporter and set the record straight. If it happens twice in a row, send a copy of the second note to the editor in charge. But avoid damaging comments and criticisms; correct the errors and do not attack the person. That reporter is likely to remain the one who covers the news from your school or system.

## Prospective Employees: Newcomers with a Need to Know

When you recruit new employees, a collection of information from the individual school or an annual report from the system works very well, as the task is to provide a general overview of the organization. In recruiting, schools and systems typically provide information on topics such as salary schedules, benefits, vacancies, application requirements, interview process, and the like. But this audience also needs information about the community—recreational opportunities, religious institutions, colleges and universities, transportation systems, rental options and properties, cultural opportunities, child care, medical facilities, access for those with disabilities, and so on. You can collect these types of information from your local governmental and business agencies, churches, and educational institutions; then add school or systemwide materials—and presto! you have a packet for recruiting. You may want to package these in a special folder with creative touches, such as a welcome letter including a phone number for questions and requests, student artwork, or pencils, pennants, pins, and notepads with the school or system emblem. (See the box "Tips for Communicating with Prospective Employees.")

## The Internal Audiences

Internal audiences include employees and students—the people whose daily business requires them to be at the school. There is no more important group when you want to build support for your school, because these audiences are perhaps your most powerful link to informal communication, brightening or tarnishing the image of the school according to what they report out in the community. And students who feel that they belong to the school and the school belongs to them are likely to support schools when they become parents and voters.

∽ **T I P S** ∽
**For Communicating with Prospective Employees**

• Collect materials from a wide variety of local sources, combine with your own materials from the school or the system, and package attractively for recruiting prospective employees.

• Coordinate your efforts with your personnel or human resources office, if appropriate.

• Remember the convenience of having a phone number for a contact person who can answer specific questions for the prospective employee.

## School Employees: The Word-of-Mouth Experts

The best public relations experts for schools are their employees, who are out in the community in all settings at all times, engaged in face-to-face communication with a variety of audiences. Upbeat word-of-mouth advertising from the people who work in schools is simply the best there is. To ensure the most positive "take" on school news, therefore, your communications plan should focus on providing accurate and timely information to employees. Further, if you want to count on spreading good news, you must take into account morale issues, trust building, and the development of two-way communication all around the organizational chart.

Employees, of course, have a variety of information needs, ranging from the usual personnel topics to updates on program changes, policies and regulations, and awards and recognitions. Beyond meeting their information needs, however, you will be wise to develop the role of employees as ambassadors of goodwill for the schools. This entails (1) a mechanism for soliciting their participation, such as invitations to become ambassadors enclosed with employment contracts or issued at the first faculty meeting of the year; (2) vehicles for communicating routinely, such as employee newsletters and recognitions; (3) internal bulletins regarding timely topics such as school board actions; and (4) inclusion of both certificated and classified employees in training sessions for understanding their role in building school support.

The inclusion of all groups of employees is very important. For example, a high school committee, trying to enhance the school's image, devoted much attention to teacher morale but later found that unrest among cafeteria employees was working against their effort. The food service workers, because their issues were not being heard, were complaining to their friends and neighbors, creating a stream of negativity in the community. Fortunately, once the omission was recognized, the committee included all groups of employees in all morale-building activities and facilitated access to the principal so that the issues could be resolved. In another case, a specific point made by an elementary principal at her first faculty and staff meeting of each year is that the school family is like any other family, in that it experiences conflicts and complaints as well as joys and accomplishments. She then requests that the conflicts and complaints come to her so that they can be resolved within the family rather than migrate onto the grapevine, where they could damage the school's image among the families it serves.

Employees typically get a great morale boost when they are recognized for their accomplishments. For example, you can send news releases about their recent degrees, promotions, awards, and honors to their hometown newspapers as well as the local ones, and to their college and university alumni associations. To make this easy and manageable, you can construct a template for such releases and a standardized memo requesting the pertinent information from the employee, including photos of the subject, so that the process is streamlined and considerate of staff time. Recognitions by the school board and news items in school and systemwide newsletters also create the "good vibes" leading to high morale. Such recognitions also increase public confidence in the qualifications of educators.

Résumé reviews provide another opportunity for positive communication with employees. Many school employees pay little attention to the development and design of their résumés; yet there are numerous calls for these documents. Of course, job searches require them, but so do grants applications, program proposals, and public appearances. If you can, offer to review existing résumés and to suggest improvements in format and content. Remember to recommend periodic updating of the résumé and maintenance on a computer file. (See the box "Tips for Communicating with School Employees.")

## Students: They're an Audience, Too

In naming audience segments, it's easy to overlook students. After all, they don't choose to be in school. They are required to attend (sometimes for reasons they can't or won't comprehend), to behave appropriately, to do their classwork and homework, and so on. But students are schools' major clients and the future supporters of the schools. Your best investment in the long run may be the resources you put into school songs, mascots, and teams; school spirit promotions; the development of positive relationships with adults; and efforts to create a sense of community in schools.

---

### ∞ T I P S ∞
### For Communicating with
### School Employees

• Provide accurate and timely information to school employees routinely and regularly. Include schedule changes, benefits information, stories about best practices, and policies and regulations.

• Keep in mind that employee morale, trusting relationships, and two-way communication will influence whether or not employees naturally spread the good news.

• Cultivate the role of goodwill ambassador for all employees. Include certificated and classified personnel in all such efforts.

• Create awareness that problems and conflicts can be solved at the school and belong there, not on the neighborhood grapevine, where they can foster discontent.

• Boost morale by sending news releases about employees' accomplishments to their hometown newspapers and alumni associations. Keep employee recognition foremost in employee newsletters. Assist the school board in recognizing employee accomplishments.

Looking to the future, you can promote school support among students in such creative and inexpensive ways as these: (1) providing a certificate of enrollment with the school colors, mascot, and date of enrollment, welcoming that student and proclaiming his or her membership in the school family forever; (2) giving each student a school pen, pencil, pennant, or drinking cup at the beginning of the school year; (3) providing color postcards of the school for sending to grandparents during Grandparents' Week; (4) providing student mentors for new enrollees; or (5) giving each student transferring to another school a wallet card with the school photo, name, address, e-mail address, and phone number, and a slogan indicating lifetime membership such as "No matter where you go, you'll always be a Mountaineer!"

Teachers know how rewarding it is to have long-term relationships with students. For example, a former student wanted to tell a teacher he was getting his doctorate and to express his appreciation for her inspiring teaching. He queried the school system's home page; the webmaster located the teacher and forwarded her school address to the former student. In another case, a former student found his high school English teacher working for a large city school system. They exchanged greetings and caught up with each other across 1,400 miles, 20 years after he had been in her English class. How can we build on such personal relationships and extend the positive connections to the school itself and to education in general?

A very powerful strategy for creating long-term support is the development of high school alumni associations. A number of forward-looking high schools have capitalized on positive relationships with their students to create these associations, using the Graduate Connection Program, a database program from Harris Publishing Company, to create their own alumni directories and mailing lists. In Eagle Rock, California, the Eagle Rock High School Alumni Association has 1,600 dues-paying members, publishes a newsletter three times a year, and awards 20 scholarships a year from a growing endowment now totaling nearly $200,000. At Governor Mifflin High School in Shillington, Pennsylvania, the alumni association has funded the purchase of equipment for the study of weather and for laboratory work with DNA. Recently 70 people from the Class of 1981 toured the school to see the changes made since they were there, and any alumnus who visits the area is invited to come in and talk with students about his or her career. In 1996, the Salem Educational Foundation and Alumni Association in Salem, Virginia, inducted 56 distinguished alumni into its Hall of Fame and immediately began planning its next induction ceremony because so many more nominations came in after the first one. This group also awarded $54,000 to 26 scholarship recipients. Even in schools where alumni associations have existed for years, the development of an alumni directory has given new life to the associations. In Fenton, Michigan, the Fenton Senior High School Alumni

Association, created 60 years ago, raised more than $75,000 in 1996, making it possible to award two $1,000 scholarships from the interest earned on the money raised. (To find out more, see information about the Harris Publishing Company in Appendix J.)
(See the box "Tips for Communicating with Students.")

## Overlaps Among the Segments

This analysis highlights the distinctive characteristics of each audience segment and, consequently, shows how you can tailor your efforts to particular needs. But the segments overlap somewhat. For example, note the commonalities between the needs of economic development offices and prospective employees. Or note the similarities between the needs of families and the needs of opinion leaders and economic development offices. Keeping track of the overlaps will help you to shape messages and to see where you can use the same news stories or news releases. In this way your efforts will pay off in reaching more than one audience and in increasing your efficiency in getting out the school's varied messages. With some advance planning, you can use one document for more than one audience—a cost-effective move.

## Audience Analysis for the Web Site

Audience analysis for Web sites and home pages requires a different approach to shaping

---

### ∞ T I P S ∞
### For Communicating with Students

- Support positive relationships with students, as you always have.
- Explore innovative methods for fostering a sense of belonging to the school and a sense of community in which each student is valued and respected and feels responsibility to contribute.
- Make school membership important—issue welcome packets, wallet cards, postcards of the building or team, and the like. Use the school mascot, school colors, and school emblems on personal items to be given at enrollment and at graduation or transfer. Be at least as creative as a fast-food chain.
- Begin an alumni association, especially if you work in a high school. Over the years, develop the alumni association as a source of support within the community.

---

messages for audience segments. The menu selections of a home page, based on existing print publications, help to meet the needs of different audiences. For example, your parent newsletter will be one selection on the menu; perhaps board meeting minutes will be another, with the employee newsletter yet another. The members of each audience segment simply self-select the information they are interested in by the topic they click on. As you design your Web site, check your menu selections to be sure you have included something for every audience segment. Of course, anyone may browse all the menu selections and stop to learn more at any point, and that's all to the good. (For guidelines, see Appendix G, "How to Create a Home Page.")

## A Note About "Spin"

In shaping messages for varied audiences, are you spinning the news? That is, if you select the most positive explanation for any occurrence or select topics so that the intended audience gets the information it needs, have you become a spin doctor? Yes, but not in the pejorative sense of the term. You may have become a more persuasive writer and much more knowledgeable about public relations, but you don't go so far as to cover up, twist the facts, or create untruths.

*Spin* is a slang word for a simple technique of persuasive writing (or other communications) in which the writer (or TV editor) chooses the information or perspective to present, selects what to emphasize or feature, and determines what to omit or downplay. Remember, these skills are taught routinely as part of the language arts curriculum. Today's pejorative connotations have occurred because, in extremes, spin means that information or perspective deemed negative to the person or organization at the center of the news is what

gets omitted, or that deliberate twists of the facts are employed to protect the image of that person or organization.

Communications work requires drawing a line between acceptable spin and indefensible spin. For example, when test scores are disappointing, your news release can include information about a new volunteer tutoring program to improve student learning, without blaming anyone or making excuses for poor performance. This shows that the school or system is not trying to cover up anything, blame the state for imposing standards, or characterize the parents as not providing what their children need for school success. Instead, the school or system is taking responsibility for the test scores by mobilizing to improve and looking toward the future, when better scores may be one result of the effort. Another suggestion is to include information about other, more laudatory achievements such as scholarships and academic awards, to show that test scores are only one measure of performance and that on other measures the school's performance is more encouraging.

Spin means giving the news a particular slant, creating the most advantageous presentation of the story or the information for the image of your school or system. That's your job. But the dishonest uses of spin risk your integrity. Loss of integrity leads to loss of credibility, which in turn brings about a tarnished image of and diminished confidence in the school or system—the very opposites of what you set out to accomplish.

## Communications Vehicles

Once you have analyzed the community at large and determined the messages each audience segment needs or wants to receive, you can begin to evaluate whether your communications plan adequately addresses these needs in terms of vehicles used for communication. For example, you may discover you are depending on local news outlets alone to convey school messages to the opinion leaders of the community. Then you may question whether media coverage alone is enough for reaching the decision makers and key communicators. Or you may realize you have no vehicle for reaching and recruiting prospective employees. Matching varied messages with varied vehicles to communicate effectively with the varied audiences in your community is an important part of any communications plan.

In teaching, you don't expect to use the same textbooks, workbooks, software, and videos with different grade levels, students of all ages and capacities, and varied subject matter. Similarly, to reach the varied audience segments in your community, you will need a variety of vehicles for carrying the many messages you want to convey. Indeed, just as in the classroom, sheer variety is a bonus, appealing to different learning styles and modalities, even when the messages are similar.

Some of the necessary vehicles or outlets are likely to be firmly established in your community, such as local TV news programs and newspapers. Other traditional outlets, such as school and parent newsletters, may need to be reviewed and renewed to increase their responsiveness, timeliness, and appeal. Other options, such as fact sheets, executive bulletins, press packets, and school information videos, may have to be started from scratch or created in response to particular situations. (For assistance, see Appendix D, "How to Develop Responsive Publications," and Appendix F, "How to Produce a School Information Video.")

In any case, it is helpful to extend your planning by developing a chart, like Figure 3.1, to be sure your communications program is reaching the varied audience segments in the community. If you've already listed the audience segments in your community, just add the vehicles you have at your disposal for reaching each segment. This process will help you to identify gaps and omissions in your own ways and means of getting the messages out.

## Breaking the Jargon Habit

No matter what vehicles you choose to convey your messages, plain language (or plain English) is the ticket for good communication with all audience segments. Educators, however, have the habit of using jargon, or "educationese," which may be confusing to others. It is easier to choose simple, direct, clear language when you examine why educators use jargon. Here are some of the influences that have led to the jargon habit:

• Professional preparation programs teach a specialized and technical vocabulary. Other

**Figure 3.1.**
**Vehicles for Reaching Varied Audiences**

| Audience | Vehicles |
|---|---|
| Students | • School spirit campaigns<br>• Systemwide honor rolls<br>• School songs, mascots, and team colors<br>• Certificates of enrollment<br>• Membership cards<br>• School promotional items<br>• Systemwide honors and awards<br>• Alumni associations |
| Parents and families | • Systemwide parents' newsletter<br>• School newsletters<br>• Systemwide newsletters for special education and gifted and talented education<br>• Superintendent's TV show<br>• PTA/PTO/PTSA newsletters<br>• Systemwide school guide or annual report<br>• Brochures about programs and services<br>• Summary of school board actions<br>• Systemwide and school home pages<br>• Fact sheets<br>• School information videos |
| Citizens and retired people | • School news items in civic group newsletters and local tabloids<br>• Local newspapers, TV, and radio<br>• Advertisements in newspapers |
| Opinion leaders or key communicators | • Superintendent's occasional letters<br>• Executive bulletins or newsletters |
| Economic development offices | • Systemwide school guide or annual report<br>• Brochures about programs and services |
| School employees | • Systemwide employee newsletter<br>• Summary of school board action<br>• Internal bulletins<br>• News releases<br>• Superintendent's TV show<br>• Systemwide Intranets and school home pages<br>• Fact sheets |
| Prospective employees | • Systemwide school guide or annual report<br>• Brochures about programs and services<br>• Promotional video for recruiting purposes<br>• Systemwide and school home pages |
| Media (and through them, the community at large) | • News releases<br>• Media alerts<br>• Photo opportunities (ops)<br>• Story plants and pitches<br>• News conferences |

professions—law, medicine, engineering, and others—have their own jargon. Jargon becomes a sort of status symbol for the professions, so it seems important.

• The use of simple words can convey the feeling of being "written down to." Sometimes people think that obscure, dense writing is good just because it *sounds* erudite.

• Textbooks with graded readability levels may have inadvertently conveyed the idea that simple language is for 1st graders. Simple language may sound *uneducated*.

• Abstract language has its uses, such as for policy statements, where flexibility in language is needed so that varying interpretations can fit what has been said rather than committing the speaker or writer to some clearly defined outcome. Clear, simple, concrete language leads to an emphasis on observable expectations and measurable results.

For a classic explanation of clear language, see *The Elements of Style* by William Strunk and E. B. White.

Whatever the reason for the jargon habit, remember this: to communicate effectively with your varied audiences, the rule for the use of jargon is "Don't!"

## The Issue of Image: Slick or Not So Slick?

School publications—print and video and Web sites—should be nice but not too nice. If they are too nice, critics will say they cost too much.

You are spending tax dollars, after all, and the public needs to see that you are carefully husbanding their money and their trust. Nor will slick publications convey school culture convincingly—school culture is not slick but very human. Teaching and learning are about active participation in an ongoing process, with daily struggles, exciting encounters, and hope for the common good and our common future. Your image of school culture needs to reflect these realities: the evolving, give-and-take nature of teaching and learning. Of course, publications should be professional, accurate in every respect, well-designed, and enticing to the audience. Managing the balance between these considerations can be tricky, but it is something you should keep in mind.

One other point: It is not wise to go to the extreme of using only student art to convey your school image. Children and teenagers are wonderful artists; and your school should display their work, framed and labeled, in hallways, classrooms, and every conceivable community venue. But budgets rarely allow for four-color printing or the most advantageous presentation of student work in print; and children themselves, especially younger students, may not be familiar with the principles of designing logos nor with the complexities of corporate images. For these tasks, find a professional or a gifted amateur designer. And when you do, or even if you get a windfall for publications, be prepared to publicize the cost of each publication and the amount of any donation.

# 4

# Creating a Positive School Climate

Image is your school's reflection in the mirror of public opinion.

You've probably noticed glossy ads or amusing commercials that are much more impressive than the stuff they advertise. Have you ever thought the company should invest more in the product and not so much in the ad? The customers would be better served, and so would the company. School patrons feel that way, too. Quality must come before hype if schools are to gain strong support from their communities. No amount of marketing can make up for a second-rate product.

Similarly, communications alone cannot convince people that your school is wonderful if they visit the campus and are not favorably impressed. The school must be as good in reality as it is in pictures and words. Does your school—the real thing—come across as first rate?

How can we tell that any organization is a quality place? Let's contrast two automobile service shops, both with personable service managers who greet customers by name. At the first shop, the service manager writes down your reasons for bringing the car in but treats you as if you don't know much about cars. The service bays are small, dark, and crowded, cluttered with used parts and greasy tools on the floor. The mechanics wear soiled coveralls, have dirty hands, and need a shave. At the other shop, the service manager consults your car's records on the computer, advises what is needed, and asks why you brought the car in. He never ridicules or makes patronizing remarks about your descriptions. The bays are well lighted and spacious, the floor is sparkling, tools are clean and in apple-pie order, and the mechanics are clean and neat. You notice that whenever you patronize the first shop, you always have to take the car back for some small adjustment within two or three days of the service. But when you take the car to the second shop, everything is properly serviced on the first trip. Which shop would get your business?

This example shows clearly how an organization's climate conveys an impression of whether the organization knows its business, focuses on its mission, and accomplishes its mission effectively and efficiently. The same is true in schools—school climate communicates whether you know your business, focus on your mission, and accomplish that mission effectively and efficiently.

School climate is not easy to measure, because it blends physical, academic, organizational, and social-emotional elements; still, every school makes an impression of one sort or another on visitors. Human beings have the ability to detect the feeling-tones of any environment they happen to be in. But you may be too familiar with your school to judge its climate. If so, put yourself in the shoes of a first-time visitor. Would you like what you see? Would the school project a positive image—a businesslike, yet student-centered atmosphere, where academics come first, supported by competence and caring? Would you want to enroll your children? Would you feel your tax dollars were well spent? Would you sense that the school is achieving its mission?

Try the first-time visitor perspective with the following two vignettes, one for an elementary school and one for a secondary school. These should prepare you for analyzing the elements of school climate later in the chapter and identifying your school's strengths and weaknesses.

## A First-Time Visitor to an Elementary School

Arriving at the school, you park in a visitor space across from the covered walkway that leads to the front door. Once under that walkway, you see for yourself how it protects students from sun and rain. Your eyes are drawn to the entrance, where flowers, azaleas, and a Japanese cherry tree welcome you.

Inside, you find yourself in a large open foyer, facing the gym. Students give you a smile as they pass by. They walk quietly, but a buzz of activity comes from every direction. In front of you, bright watercolor paintings reflect the study of the sea just completed by the 4th grade. There's an information center off to the left, where you find brochures about every classroom. A large open scrapbook holds color photos of school activities, and another binder is full of the year's collection of news releases. A bulletin board invites everyone to attend the next PTA meeting, mostly to hear the chorus perform but also because new curriculum standards will be explained. Further to the left there is a display of kindergarten art—potato prints with white designs on colored construction paper. The sounds of bouncing balls and excited cheers come from the gym. Glancing in, you see students, 5th graders probably, running relays. The teacher holds his whistle, watches the students closely, and checks his watch.

Then you spot the sign saying "Office," pointing to the right. Opening the office door, you are greeted by smiling secretaries. One leaves her desk and comes to the counter, asking "May I help you?" She notifies the principal that you've arrived, and the principal emerges from her office. After she greets you, you pose for a snapshot, which will go up on the office bulletin board. Unhurried, charming, projecting warmth and decisiveness, the principal gives you a tour of the school.

It's an ordinary school day—the library/media center is filled with youngsters using books; the computer lab has a child in every seat, eyeing the screen intently; in the classrooms, the lessons of the day are moving forward. Everywhere the school is sparkling clean, and student work is displayed. The principal fills you in on the details: this class, that class, the new teacher, the valued old-timer in her last year, the school's initiative to teach citizenship.

Throughout the school, you and the principal are hailed with big smiles. You notice that several classrooms have more than one adult at work with the children. The extras are faithful parent volunteers, who assist the teachers in a hundred different ways. You pass the music room and stop to hear children practicing the songs for the PTA program—folk songs from many cultures. Their faces are shining with the joy of singing well and knowing it.

A peek into the teachers' workroom shows one or two teachers at the photocopier and another writing busily at the table. There's a bulletin board over the table; the principal explains this is where the employees post snapshots of their own children and families, their dogs and cats and hobbies. "It helps us to get to know each other as human beings, not just as workers," she says. "It's great for the parents, too, for the same reason—they know we're 'real people.' "

As you stroll back toward the office, you notice students and adults in twos and threes spread out around the cafeteria. The children are being tutored in math by men and women from a neighborhood bank, a school partner. You can't judge the effects on the children's skills with one glance, but the eagerness in their eyes clearly shows the benefits of extra adult attention. The principal explains that on the last Friday of every month, the bank employees return to receive deposits to the children's savings accounts and add in the interest they are accruing. . . .

Preparing to leave, you begin to understand that this school is a good place for children. Here you see support and space, challenge and comfort for the personal effort of growing up, becoming a contributor and a citizen, and stretching one's talent and ambition as far as possible. You sense this school is achieving its mission—educating its students to become competent and responsible members of a class, a community, a nation, and the human race.

## A First-Time Visitor to a Secondary School

When you park in the visitor section of the school parking area, the first thing you see is the main entry. Even across the parking lot, you can easily spot the front door, because all the sidewalks lead to it. The main entry is located under the point where the wings of the building come together. It's comforting to be able to locate the main door because the building is large and daunting to a first-time visitor. Once inside, you find yourself in a large atrium, spacious and inviting, with a number of chairs and wooden benches in conversational groupings. A window wall on the far side looks out onto a courtyard, full of plants and small trees. The large display case in front of the office contains self-portraits by students in art class; on either side are displays of Revolutionary War documents and artifacts. A smaller display case invites parents to sign up as volunteers and exhibits photos of smiling parents at work in the school. Also displayed are school mugs, pennants, folders, and the like, offered at the student-run school store. Signs point down the hallways to the library/media center and auditorium on the left and the cafeteria on the right.

Suddenly you are approached by a smiling man who offers his hand and greets you: "Welcome to our school! May I help you?" He introduces himself as the principal and says he'll take you through the school, just as the bell rings and the halls fill with chattering students.

The principal excuses himself, saying you are not to go away, and begins greeting students. "Morning, Jamie. How's it going today? . . . Ah, Lydia, how are things on the home front? How's math lately? . . . Tomas, great job you did last Friday night. Proud of you, young man. . . . Missed you last week, Deirdre. Hope you're feeling better now." The students respond with smiles and quips back to him. He keeps on working the crowd until the end of the break, when the halls begin to clear again. The students who had stopped to talk or rest in the atrium lounge get up, straighten their books, and move to their next classes, a few loud comments and boisterous moves punctuating the flow of young people to their destinations.

Soon the principal is guiding you to the library/media center. You walk around, noticing how busy everyone is: students checking the online catalog, a student assistant shelving books, another checking books out, and students scattered around the study carrels, working on various assignments. The librarian is helping a small group of students learn to use search engines on the Internet. You notice an extensive videotape collection and, on the floor, racks of paperback trade books appealing to teens. On your way out of the library, you notice an exhibit of original book jackets, created by English literature students for new and old classics. The library secretary waves from the office cubicle and the principal waves back, then notices a parent volunteer shelving books. He greets her, introduces you, and she tells you how special the school is. "Parents love this school. We know we are welcome. We can remain a part of our kids' education here." The principal beams. "Parents do so much for our students," he says. "Whenever we call for help, they are ready to give us what we need."

Back in the hallway, you make a quick survey of classrooms. In this wing you are in the social studies department. There's an exhibit on Ancient Greece, featuring student-designed posters showing the influence of Greece on American architecture. Another features 18th-century drawings of the town matched with contemporary photos, revealing changes since the American Revolution—a way of making history come alive. Inside the classrooms, you see various types of instruction. Here's a teacher lecturing about Ben Franklin's days in Paris, while the students take notes. In another classroom, a video episode from "Eyes on the Prize" is being shown to illustrate a study of contemporary issues. In another, pairs of students are being called for conferences at the teacher's desk, presenting their outlines for papers on the world's economy before and after the American Revolution. In the math department, you see students at computers practicing math skills, another group solving algebra problems at chalkboards with the teacher coaching them, and still another class hearing a lecture on fractals, with references to their study of botany.

And so it goes through the other academic departments, the gym and auditorium, and the outdoor playing fields. In the auditorium you notice ramps to the stage—a wheelchair-accessible stage! On the playing fields, you see half a dozen wheelchair students circling the track. Seems that everyone participates in some physical activity here. . . .

After your tour is finished, you thank the principal and slowly walk toward the parking lot, feeling renewed hope in America's future. You feel confident that these students are growing toward personal responsibility, good character, academic achievement, and mature physical and emotional development. They have abundant adult guidance, yet independence and self-discipline are evident. They'll be ready for higher education or the workplace, whichever comes first. This school has its act together.

## Analyzing Your School Climate

To assist you in analyzing how your school may look to a first-time visitor, try completing the School Climate Checklist at the end of this chapter (Figure 4.1, p. 42). Better still, use the checklist as an activity at a staff meeting, so that the entire faculty and staff can contribute their input. Then you or your group can arrive at your own school profile, identifying areas to take pride in and areas needing further work. These areas, in turn, may indicate where you need to add goals or strategies to your communications plan.

### Translating Areas for Improvement into Goals and Strategies

If your school climate profile has revealed a glaring omission in what your school is doing to create a positive climate, now's the time to share the profile and collect ideas from the faculty and staff about improving the situation. For example, you may have realized that parents and citizens have no real source of information about the credentials of the faculty and staff other than the grapevine. You may want to discuss how to remedy this omission. Should your school provide a directory with capsule biographies of all faculty and staff? Or would a newsletter supplement fill the need? Should photographs of faculty and staff be included? Perhaps someone points out that phone manners at the school are not the best. What is the best way to train everyone in good phone manners? Or you may find that no one has invited VIPs to visit the school recently, nor sent them school newsletters. How can you develop an up-to-date mailing list of VIPs? If parents have complained about misspelled words on notes going home, what procedures will ensure this never happens again?

When you add to an existing overall strategic plan, consider whether you need an entirely new and separate goal or can remedy the omission by adding strategies to existing goals.

## Translating Areas for Congratulations into Celebration

If you find your school is performing exceptionally well in any area, it may be instructive to think back and recount together as a faculty and staff what was involved in developing such outstanding performance. Reliving the development of every action that led to exemplary performance in, say, implementing a partnership program or beautifying the school entrance can boost staff morale and encourage further commitment to a positive climate overall. Praiseworthy achievements by faculty and staff deserve recognition and appreciation. A packet of supplies, personalized note pads, punch and cookies—whatever will show appreciation to employees for a job well done is a good idea at any juncture. Never miss a chance to celebrate your successes!

## When Reality Lives Up to Advertising

When you've made your school as appealing in reality as it is on paper, you will enjoy an extra dose of confidence about what newcomers find when they visit and what repeat visitors have come to expect. The support for your school will grow stronger every time school patrons tell you about their positive impressions; after all, they'll be telling their friends and neighbors the same. Awareness of the importance of school climate will help you to foster an atmosphere that makes everyone feel comfortable in the school and confident about what is happening there (maybe not just confident but *proud*). Your school reality will be first rate, and you won't have to worry about a product that doesn't live up to its advertising.

## Figure 4.1.
## School Climate Checklist

The following elements of school climate are grouped into 11 categories. Consider each element, and place a check mark in the space next to each one found in your school. Add up the check marks to determine your school's score in each category. (Feel free to include additional elements your school has created.)

**1. First Impressions and Signs of Welcome**

**(11 points possible)** _____ **OUR SCORE**

☐ Grounds are clean and landscaped, with seasonal flowers or displays.

☐ Building and outdoor facilities are well maintained and in good condition.

☐ Outside lights are on for safety during night meetings and parent conferences.

☐ Marquee is up-to-date; message is informative and spelled correctly.

☐ Convenient parking is provided, with areas for visitors clearly marked.

☐ Interior of building is sparkling clean: windows, floors, walls, furniture, equipment.

☐ Signage is clear and friendly, and includes welcome and directions to office and to check-in area.

☐ Office staff are always warm, welcoming, polite, and attentive.

☐ Prompt response follows patrons' requests for service or information.

☐ Well-organized atmosphere inspires confidence in patrons.

☐ All staff are trained in use of helpful and friendly telephone manners at all times.

**2. Appropriate Environment**

**(9 points possible)** _____ **OUR SCORE**

☐ Environment is safe, secure, drug-free, and focused on academics.

☐ Excellent discipline, with clear expectations for student conduct, is in evidence.

☐ Students are happy, engaged in activities, with age-appropriate levels of self-discipline.

☐ Warm, caring, student-centered climate is calm and orderly, with a "buzz" of conversation and activity.

☐ Students with disabilities are included in activities and classrooms; access is ensured.

☐ Student work is displayed in hallways, classrooms, and common areas.

☐ Bulletin boards are up-to-date, attractive, illustrating program content/student work.

☐ Predictable routine is balanced by exciting events.

☐ Many cultures are represented in displays, both to establish student sense of belonging and to accurately depict the world's diversity.

**3. Information for Parents and Citizens**

**(20 points possible)** _____ **OUR SCORE**

☐ Schedules, rules, and policies are readily available in print.

☐ School newsletters and announcements are color-coded to get attention.

☐ Brochures are available to explain specific programs.

☐ Happy-grams or other personal notes are sent to parents frequently.

☐ Phone calls to parents are made often, and early when problems occur.

☐ In any crisis, letters giving the facts are sent to parents that day.

☐ Parenting workshops are provided and publicized, with child care available.

☐ Curriculum or grade-level meetings are held often and at different times of day and evening.

☐ School information video is available and up-to-date.

☐ School Web site is available, publicized, up-to-date, and informative.

☐ PTA/PTO/PTSA membership is encouraged; child care is provided during meetings.

☐ Parent mentors are provided for parents new to the school.

☐ All levels of participation and involvement are welcomed—no parent is made to feel inadequate or bad because he or she cannot volunteer.

☐ Homework hot line is available.

☐ Before- and after-school child care is provided, or there is an abundance of after-school activities (both athletics and academic activities) for older students.

☐ Parents' needs are assessed annually.

☐ Textbook review opportunities are publicized.

☐ Printed material is provided in languages other than English.

☐ Translators are provided upon request.

☐ Alternative forms of materials are available for the disabled upon request.

## 4. Staff Spirit and Morale

**(5 points possible)** _____ **OUR SCORE**

☐ Staff are valued for their contributions; administrators routinely express their appreciation.

☐ Staff concerns are dealt with promptly, privately, and cheerfully.

☐ Staff are trained for their role as ambassadors in the community.

☐ There is an ongoing effort to create and maintain spirit of teamwork and community.

☐ Staff mentors are provided for new staff members.

## 5. Staff Professionalism

**(9 points possible)** _____ **OUR SCORE**

☐ Focus on instructional program is recognized as the top priority and is widely accepted as the mission of the school.

☐ Instructional resources are available and abundant.

☐ High expectations for performance are well known.

☐ Staff development is available for curriculum demands and teaching techniques, as are moral support and mentoring.

☐ Brochures about each staff member are displayed in foyer, including description of staff member's responsibilities, summary of credentials, and invitation to parents and citizens to visit.

☐ Staff honors, such as new degrees awarded, are recognized in school newsletters.

☐ Business cards are provided for all staff, in generous amounts.

☐ Accuracy of spelling, grammar, and punctuation in newsletters, notes, and happy-grams is ensured.

☐ Accessibility of principal is ensured; confidentiality and problem solving are prevalent.

## 6. Conferencing Techniques

**(8 points possible)** _____ **OUR SCORE**

☐ Conferences are scheduled at parents' convenience.

☐ Conferences are scheduled for "conference days," and as needed individually.

☐ Parents and staff members may initiate conferences as needed.

☐ Staff are trained in conferencing techniques.

☐ Students participate in conferences as needed; this option is highly recommended for 4th grade and above.

☐ Follow-up strategies are agreed upon and listed at end of conference.

☐ Checkpoints to assess effectiveness of follow-up strategies for improvement are identified.

☐ Checkpoints are always reported back to parents; strategies are assessed and adjusted as necessary.

## 7. Volunteers and Partners

**(6 points possible)**     \_\_\_\_\_ **OUR SCORE**

☐ Parent and caregiver volunteers are welcome and busy with assignments.

☐ "Visitor" tags are provided for all visitors, as are picture ID tags for volunteers.

☐ Community partners are active in mentoring, tutoring, beautification, career days, and so forth.

☐ Check-in procedures and duties are spelled out.

☐ Appreciation for volunteers and partners is abundant, with recognition in school newsletter, personal notes, teas and receptions, special days, notes from students, photo boards, and library displays.

☐ Student volunteers serve the community in nursing homes and in other capacities.

## 8. Broader Community

**(8 points possible)**     \_\_\_\_\_ **OUR SCORE**

☐ All staff bring community issues to the principal (issues management process).

☐ All staff act as ambassadors for the school.

☐ Power of the grapevine is harnessed.

☐ Community groups feel free to approach the principal (and do).

☐ Principal participates in civic groups, church activities, athletic associations, and the like.

☐ Entire community is invited for school events such as picnics, holiday celebrations, drama productions, art shows, musical presentations, science fairs, technology exhibits, athletic events, honors programs, and other activities.

☐ Retired people and grandparents receive special invitations to visit and have lunch, read to students, exhibit their collections, judge art shows, and so forth.

☐ High-achieving graduates are invited back to give greetings or make addresses, talk with students, and encourage students to study hard and strive for great accomplishments.

## 9. News Media

**(11 points possible)**     \_\_\_\_\_ **OUR SCORE**

☐ Staff member(s) is (are) trained in writing news releases.

☐ News releases are sent in advance of events.

☐ Responsibility for calling reporters and editors is clear and active.

☐ List of local media contacts is maintained and kept current.

☐ Principal(s) is (are) trained as media spokesperson(s).

☐ Responsibilities are clear for who appears on camera, depending on the story.

☐ Calls from reporters and editors are always returned in a timely manner.

☐ Parental permission is obtained before any student can be filmed or photographed.

☐ Crisis communications and safe schools plans are updated; staff are trained in both annually.

☐ Binder of procedures is maintained in office for easy use by staff member or volunteer.

☐ Letters of appreciation are always sent to reporters and editors.

## 10. Opinion Leaders at All Levels

**(5 points possible)**     \_\_\_\_\_ **OUR SCORE**

☐ Opinion leaders are invited to visit often, to read to students, to speak to groups, and so forth.

☐ Student artwork and thank-you letters are sent to all visitors promptly after their visits.

☐ Student artwork and other samples of work, with letters from students, are sent to opinion leaders during American Education Week, Teacher Appreciation Week, Math Month, Reading Month, and so forth.

☐ School newsletters are sent to opinion leaders, especially with news of their visits.

☐ Photos are taken of all VIPs during their visits, preferably with students and in classrooms; complimentary copies are sent to them; other copies are exhibited in school and offered to newspapers.

## 11. Students—The Future of School Support

**(10 points possible)** _____ **OUR SCORE**

☐ Student school spirit is cultivated, through such means as school songs, mascots, pencils, and pennants.

☐ Membership cards or certificates of membership in the school community are provided for all students upon enrollment.

☐ Goodie bags of school supplies are provided for new students.

☐ Lifetime membership wallet cards are provided when students leave, with school address, phone number, and Web site address.

☐ Buddies and sponsors are provided for new students.

☐ Ongoing efforts are made to promote sense of belonging to the school, to show caring and respect for each student (birthday and get-well cards, for example), to provide appropriate adult guidance and optimum opportunities for that student's growth and development.

☐ In high schools, alumni association is established and maintained; class reunions are held frequently, and follow-up surveys are conducted.

☐ In high schools, spirit stores offer items like pennants, binders, caps, and T-shirts with the school logo(s).

☐ Students are recognized for a variety of exemplary accomplishments in a hall of fame in commons area, in newsletters, by having lunch with the principal, and so forth.

☐ Bumper stickers emphasize sense of community and belonging, not just honor roll students.

## Tallying Your School's Scores: Determining Your School Profile

1. First Impressions and Signs of Welcome _____ out of 11
2. Appropriate Environment _____ out of 9
3. Information for Parents and Citizens _____ out of 20
4. Staff Spirit and Morale _____ out of 5
5. Staff Professionalism _____ out of 9
6. Conferencing Techniques _____ out of 8
7. Volunteers and Partners _____ out of 6
8. Broader Community _____ out of 8
9. News Media _____ out of 11
10. Opinion Leaders at All Levels _____ out of 5
11. Students—The Future of School Support _____ out of 10

**Total Possible Points: 102**

**OUR SCORE:** _____

## Areas for Improvement: Work on These

Write down the three categories that show the greatest gap between your score and the highest possible score. These are areas your school needs to work on.

1. _____
2. _____
3. _____

## Areas for Congratulations: Take Pride in These

Write down the three categories that show the smallest gap between your score and the highest possible score. These are areas your school can take pride in.

1. _____
2. _____
3. _____

# 5

# Linking Communications to
# Community Relations

Building support for schools is about building relationships—*positive* relationships.
Communication is the cultivation of those positive relationships.

In the realm of community relations, face-to-face communication—that highly prized commodity—is the order of the day. You can capitalize on these face-to-face interactions in your overall communications program, and without undue effort. The idea is never to lose a chance to strengthen communication with important constituents. Here's another important principle: Never lose a chance to keep your ears open for hearing what issues are on the minds of the public. Effective communication is a two-way exchange—sending messages out and listening to what people have to say.

Just think how valued and valuable face-to-face interactions are! PTA/PTO/PTSA meetings, parenting workshops, community forums, partnership programs, civic club meetings, and the like—all bring educators and their constituents "up close and personal." Once you recognize the value of such meetings, you can easily prepare to use them as extra chances to communicate. Keep in mind, of course, that no person can *control* the conversations and exchanges that occur during meetings and events.

## Informal Connections Between Schools and Community

To begin with, there is an abundant supply of natural informal connections between schools and the community. As citizens within their own communities, educators typically will be making all sorts of extracurricular contributions—coaching teams, teaching Sunday school, volunteering on Earth Day, collecting for charitable campaigns, working night jobs, and serving on boards and committees for churches and civic organizations. In these interactions, educators will be talking about their schools, just as anyone talks about work, children, and family. The guiding thought is: *People will talk, but what will they say?* If school employees are to be positive, there are important elements in organizational climate to take into account.

## Organizational Climate and the Grapevine

As someone interested in building support for schools, you are not the only person responsible for establishing and maintaining organizational climate. The school board, superintendent, central office administrators, and principals usually set the tone and direction for the entire system. Still, you can examine the presence or absence of certain aspects of organizational climate to predict just how positive or negative the grapevine may be. Then, in your issues-management capacity, you may suggest certain improvements to your administrator. What's more, your analysis will help you determine the proactive steps you can take to link community relations and communications.

To assist in your investigation of organizational climate, here's a list of elements affecting the grapevine:

• *Trust in the leadership.* Trust doesn't happen in a hurry. Trust is a long-term growth stock strengthened by mutual respect, fair dealings, and responsibility. To develop trust in their leaders, employees must see the leaders engage in consistent acts of integrity, fairness, and compassion, without abuses of power—over time. When the leaders return that trust, showing respect and appreciation for employees, organizational climate improves across the board. Without trust flowing up and down the organizational chart, fear and uncertainty increase, and the grapevine turns sour. But with mutual trust, the grapevine tends to be positive.

• *High employee morale.* Employees who feel respected, valued, and important—especially because they feel the boss recognizes their individual contributions to an enterprise of significance—will show positive feelings in their attitudes and conversations. Certainly, high employee morale and job satisfaction are important for many reasons, not just for their benefits in community relations and communications. In healthy organizations, high morale and job satisfaction lead to increased hard work, productivity, and commitment to the organization. If, on the other hand, employees feel ignored, denigrated, or attacked, the organization will lose the momentum of their commitment, and the grapevine will bear bitter news.

• *Confidence in the professional ability and commitment of administrators.* Competent professionals—those who set appropriate direction for the school or system and address day-to-day problems effectively—will find their employees have confidence in them, and the grapevine will blossom with good reports. But if employees perceive their leaders as merely ambitious for further advancement or as just marking time, they will become cynical, feeling betrayed. Unfortunately, their talk out in the community will reflect such negative emotions.

• *Acknowledgment of the role of employees as ambassadors of goodwill.* When leaders proactively cultivate the role of employees as voices for the schools, they encourage a cumulative force for developing support for education. With this acknowledgment, employees are likely to realize their value as insiders in the school system. They will feel trusted and responsible. Even in a crisis, they will be loyal to the organization and will protect it.

• *Informative internal communications.* To serve well as ambassadors of goodwill, employees need accurate and up-to-date information to share in the community. In addition to updates on curriculum, testing, athletics, and the like, they need to know who does what, so they can answer the questions of their friends and neighbors about such topics as special education services, disciplinary policies and procedures, instructional materials, and complaint processes in general. This means that organizational changes and the names of newly hired employees, as well as school board actions and administrative decisions, need to be communicated broadly and officially. This also means that employees' questions need to be answered

promptly. If administrators guard information too closely, employees will not be able to help their friends and neighbors solve problems, simply because they lack timely and reliable information. Because employees feel powerless and helpless in such situations, lack of information in turn can increase negative feelings about the workplace.

Overall morale and attitude within the schools will thus be conveyed to the community in hundreds of small interactions. These *are* the grapevine. You may be able to influence organizational climate—certainly a lively program of internal communications is important in that regard. However, informal interactions don't lend themselves to control. You can't kill the grapevine, but, if you really work at it, sour grapes may turn to sweet ones.

## Connecting Communications to Ongoing Programs

Ongoing programs in community relations, such as interagency collaboration with social services departments, school-business partnerships, and parenting education, are communications events in and of themselves. They aren't *just* communications events—they have their own purposes. For example, consider a workshop held at the public library to show young parents how to prepare their preschoolers for 1st grade. This kind of session has goals and objectives that go beyond those of a communications plan. But the manner of the presenter at the workshop and the information conveyed to parents will reinforce the positive image of the schools—or not.

So these events are integral to an overall communications program, even if they are not the primary focus of the plan and even if they are the responsibility of a different administrator. Why? The communications plan gets an extra boost if the presenter also distributes copies of the parent newsletter, or an invitation from a preschool PTA, or a flyer from the health department, for example. It's such extras that the remainder of this chapter brings out— linkages that will boost communications as well as community relations.

## Parents, Families, and Parent Groups: Focusing on Student Achievement

Contacts with parents and families are overwhelmingly important in community relations and communications. Parental participation encompasses many levels, and all levels must be honored and encouraged if educators are to achieve (1) the involvement of parents that improves children's achievement and (2) the long-term goal of continuous parental support for schools.

Naturally, administrators need to communicate with parents and family members as individuals, as well as with organized parent *groups*. Indeed, when beset with demands from the special education advisory committee, the gifted education advisory committee, and the

PTA/PTO/PTSA, it's instructive to recall that many parents and caregivers either do not find adequate voice or representation in formal groups or have responsibilities that prevent their taking an active role in such organizations.

The most vocal and active parents and caregivers contribute much to the schools in volunteer hours, support, and demands for services. Other families may not have the luxury of such time commitments and may have to limit their involvement in school activities. However, even when time and resources are in short supply, you can depend on parents and caregivers to be deeply concerned about their children, to want to know what's going on at school, and to need accurate information for making good decisions about their children's education. *All* parents, even those whose needs and concerns may not be expressed as often or as forcefully as those of the more active parents, are important. Thus, it is essential to address the needs of all parents for reliable information, even when they are absent from PTA/PTO/PTSA meetings or community forums. Remember that parents, caregivers, and their families are also taxpayers and voters.

Depending on the size and the resources of the school or system, the superintendent may designate a staff person to handle parent liaison responsibilities. The person responsible will need to cultivate both sides of the communications loop—the giving out of information and the taking in of parent opinions, preferences, and ideas. Again, as a good listener, the parent liaison staff member serves as part of your issues management effort. Input from parents should be routinely fed into your superintendent's regular briefings or communicated according to his or her personal preference.

## Parent Education Programs: Addressing Specific Interests

Schools and school systems routinely offer a variety of parent education programs: parenting workshops, college nights, school readiness sessions for parents of preschool children, and so on. These formal occasions are made to order for strengthening communications in general, as well as for presenting specific topics of great interest. The feature of the occasion—the session or workshop or meeting—will be given its own structure by the presenters; if the presenters are employees or community volunteers or private contractors, they can be coached ahead of time about how to handle parent concerns and inquiries.

Each program can also serve as a time to distribute extra copies of parent and family newsletters, information about child care before and after school, dates and places for summer school registration, schedules for upcoming events, including news shows on community cable TV, and other such official information of interest to families. When time and resources permit, administrators can make brief appearances; they can welcome the audience, introduce the presenters, or be introduced in their administrative roles, for

example. Whatever the role, it's the personal contact that counts, so that parents in attendance get to know administrators. And the personal contacts really pay off in community support when administrators directly address parent questions and concerns and get back to the person who asked the question with good information. You may facilitate this two-way exchange by keeping track of parent requests and questions and routing them to appropriate staff members, then ensuring that timely responses come back to the persons asking the questions.

## School Volunteer Programs: Connecting Schools with Parents and Citizens

As a rule, the PTA/PTO/PTSA is the sponsor of each school's parent volunteers and takes charge of the program, including recruitment, orientation, training, and evaluation, in a nicely decentralized manner. A connecting link between the central office parent liaison and the PTA officers is effective, but it is not at all necessary to assume the management of parent and community volunteers when experienced PTA/PTO/PTSA members are adept at this task. Certain useful guidelines can be supplied by the National Parent-Teacher Association in Chicago or by state-level parent-teacher associations, if they are not available locally (see Appendix J, "Resources").

Important communications links are the annual start-up and recognition events typically organized by the PTA/PTO/PTSA. Attendance at these events is mandatory for administrators who want to show their support and gratitude. The value of recognitions cannot be overemphasized, for the message to volunteers who receive recognition for their work with students is that of appreciation and inclusion. Many schools and systems provide badges, incentive gifts, volunteer news in newsletters, recognition ceremonies, and occasional social hours with refreshments.

In addition to parent volunteers, schools and systems often recruit community volunteers from all walks of life. Retired people, military units, civic organizations, and service clubs are often good sources of such volunteers; these groups possess a multitude of talents and abilities to share with students. Just as with parent volunteers, the programs they sustain will require some structure for management and recognition for their donated time.

## School-Business-Military Partnerships: Exchanging Expertise and Information

In a large system, an administrator will likely be charged with the responsibility for managing school-business partnerships. In a smaller system, this duty may be given to someone who already has a full plate of responsibilities, either school principals or someone at the central office. Whatever the case, a structured program of partnerships is a valuable part of community relations and a major source of support for the schools. And the partnership coordinator or administrator in charge can make a special point of helping partners get answers to their questions and voice their opinions about school concerns.

In the early days of the "adopt-a-school program," as it was first called, schools and businesses and military units formed alliances in a rather casual and informal way. At the time educators were hearing much from policymakers and the media about the need for closer ties with the business community so that high school graduates would be better prepared for the workplace. Schools would gain, so the story went, by involving businesspeople in daily educational activities, so that they could see for themselves the nature and condition of schooling in their communities. Without a doubt, these benefits have accrued from the close involvement of businesses and schools.

Over time, however, as the movement matured, new standards were set, focusing on student achievement as the purpose of partnerships. These standards lift partnerships above the level of thinly disguised marketing efforts on the part of businesses. Schools that once wanted businesses to provide little more than incentive coupons for student attendance have found that business partners can also offer tutoring, mentoring, hands-on experiences in construction, internships in offices—in other words, a variety of experiences that influence student learning and attitude. The partnership office in your state department of education can tell you what partnership standards exist in your state. Or contact the National Association of Partners in Education (see Appendix J) for valuable information about forming and strengthening school partnerships.

Along with striving to meet standards, certain formal steps are recommended as a matter of course. The school and the partner agree from the outset on what the intent and shape of the partnership will be: one-on-one tutoring in basic skills, career counseling, banking services in the school lobby once a week, student internships at the business site, and so on. Once agreement is reached and expectations are clarified, the partnership is formalized with a certificate for both parties and a public ceremony at the school, accompanied by an appropriate celebration, such as a performance by students or simple refreshments.

Keep in mind that partners are not always chosen for the benefits they bestow on the students; sometimes the students provide benefits to the partner. For example, when a school adopts a nursing home and the students perform holiday music, visit with the residents, and send them letters and artwork, they are learning much about becoming responsible citizens and contributing to a sense of community in the larger world.

In all these partnership offerings, so much in feeling tones and information is exchanged, all in face-to-face interaction. To follow up such interactions, try to provide extra copies of school newsletters at partnership events, and be sure to include all partners on the newsletter mailing list. It's also a good idea to send all news releases to your school partners and to provide small gifts, student letters, and student artwork as tokens of appreciation.

## Church, Community, and Civic Groups and Ethnic Associations: Linkages for Listening

One simple strategy is to encourage or to ensure that each central office administrator takes on the role of liaison with various community constituents. Central office administrators who serve on boards and committees of community, church, and civic groups and ethnic associations are able to convey accurate information about the schools, dispel or confirm rumors, and explain circumstances on the spot. As they listen to people's concerns, they also serve the superintendent's issue management approach, for they convey what's "on the street" to the superintendent when they return to the office after attendance at regular meetings. They can demonstrate the system's responsiveness by following up on questions and concerns and then letting the citizen know what to do next. (See the section "Issues Management" in Chapter 8.)

To formalize this strategy, you can compile a definitive list of organizations and consider how each will be served. You can match the organizations with the names of administrators who already have a commitment to certain ones. Just fill in the gaps by assigning other administrators as liaisons to the remainder. You'll no doubt have a sense of which organizations have major influence on public opinion in your community, and you can concentrate on those if there are not enough central office administrators to cover all the organizations on your list. Depending on personal preference, some low-key way of reporting issues and topics to the superintendent—e-mail or notes or memos—should be indicated, to be sure of benefiting from the issues management loop.

## Governmental Bodies: Linkages with Decision Makers

School systems must necessarily create and maintain close ties with various governmental bodies—local, state, and national. For school systems without fiscal independence, school leaders must establish many points of contact with the governing bodies who eventually, if reluctantly, fund the budget. These points of contact and their modes of operating will typically be directed by the superintendent and school board. For this reason, governmental liaison roles are usually a central office function. However, many principals also maintain close ties with their local elected officials, and many of those officials treasure their connections to the schools.

Various methods of monitoring the state legislature, Congress, and federal agencies and offices enable local school leaders to keep their fingers on the pulse of the policymakers. Most of these monitoring activities, which may include outright lobbying on the part of the

larger or more affluent school districts, require specialized skills. Your professional association may be an excellent source of information about these roles. Information picked up by those who represent the school system is a valuable component of the issues management loop, even though it may not always pertain to a local matter. Knowing what is going on in the state house, for example, enables the superintendent and school board to watch developments and forecast possible responses before any action is necessary. Similarly, knowing what is going on in local government helps all educators to stay abreast of issues and influence decision making close to home.

On the state and national scenes, various professional organizations, such as teachers' associations and principals' associations, provide valuable services in monitoring developments, tracking issues, and guiding discussion. They also distribute timely information to their membership, and they often provide recommendations about policies and policymaking at the various levels. (For sources of assistance in tracking policy directions, see Appendix J.)

Perhaps the governmental activity closest to the students, however, is that provided by local social service agencies. Many children and youth are served by social service staffers, who are a special sort of caregiver and a special sort of family. This is where interagency collaboration comes in. The school system needs to have its representatives get involved with the social service agencies serving children and youth, just as it needs liaisons to community groups and civic organizations. Administrators should meet regularly with the various social service agencies. When they do, both schools and social services benefit. Both come to understand the scope of each other's work, to communicate fully about the needs of students and families, and to provide extra efforts to address those needs. This interaction pays off by increasing parental involvement in the schools, improving attendance and attitude, and helping children and youth to become successful students and productive citizens despite their present needs for social services. As you work with social service agencies serving children and youth, you can add the names and addresses of interested staffers to your mailing lists, invite them to school performances and classrooms, and include them in discussions of curriculum changes, new assessments, behavior and discipline expectations, and the like.

## Professional Associations: Finding Common Ground with Employees

School systems typically maintain cordial but guarded relationships with the various employee organizations, such as principals' associations, secretaries' associations, teachers' associations, and the like. Occasionally these loose relationships cause consternation, because of the nonspecific links with the upper administration and the school board and the inevitable salary and workplace negotiations that arise. However, working within extant policies and guidelines, a wise administration will include all professional associations in the communications loop to ensure their members receive up-to-date information about developments, direction, and issues.

This inclusion can be quite simple: an offer to provide copies of newsletters for a meeting or complimentary copies of a pertinent video program. Such simple acts may be fraught with conflict when it's budget time or negotiations are in process; but when such adversarial situations are past, this link becomes another manifestation of developing job satisfaction and high employee morale within the school and system. Further, the emphasis on professionalism within each employee association will serve the school system well in its efforts to enhance productivity and contribute to the community's overall quality of life. In other words, professional conduct is a plus in helping the school system focus on its mission and achieve its purposes; therefore, associations that promote professional standards are an asset to the school system and need to be kept in the communications loop.

## Benefits of Linkages

The foregoing suggestions, which emphasize how to link communications efforts with community relations work, do not address the goals and objectives of each kind of community relations program. I have left that to the literature on each type of program. Certainly each program mentioned here has terrific value on its own, whether or not the links with communications are formed. However, if you can form those links between community relations and communications, your school or system will realize benefits such as these:

• You will increase face-to-face communications with all constituents of the schools. This is a good outcome in itself, because all print, video, and electronic communications merely complement face-to-face interactions. The larger the district, the more value you can add by linking communications with community relations activities.

• You will strengthen your own formal communications plan and program, reaching both more audiences and more people with the messages you need to get out; this strength will be reflected in your annual evaluation of the program.

• You will increase the perception of coordination and responsiveness to the community; that is, people will perceive that the system "has its act together," rather than having a group of educators whose left hands don't know what their right hands are doing.

• You will improve the system's *actual*, not just perceived, responsiveness to its clients and constituents when you prepare your fellow employees to answer constituents' questions; this is both a matter of improving the system's present image and of improving long-term community support for public education.

• You will greatly strengthen your issues management approach, because listening to the community will enable you to forward issues and topics from constituents to the school board, the superintendent, and the principal; you will bolster your formal approach with the power of informal communications.

# 6

# Spotlighting the Good News: Media Liaisons

Only the sunny hours . . .

—SEEN ON A SUNDIAL

In small school districts, the superintendent is easily visible in the community and is able to meet most demands for information and community relations more or less single-handedly. Occasionally someone in the central administration will assist with communications tasks, possibly on a part-time basis. Larger districts commonly have a central office staff for communications, although the staff may be quite small. But even the largest school systems are not likely to employ sufficient staff to meet the community's needs for information and the entire system's needs for promotion, given today's widespread budget constraints. Suppose you have 50–60 schools and 8–10 central office departments, all needing news releases, special events planning, employee recognitions, and so on. Two or three central office staffers are not likely to be able to address such broad needs,

especially while managing crisis communications, writing speeches for the superintendent, preparing budget summaries, assisting with school board recognitions, and preparing newsletters.

What to do? Organize a media liaison program.

A media liaison is a school employee who acts as publicity chair for that school. He or she prepares news releases; promotes media attention for programs, events, and honors; and assists the principal in informing the community about what is happening at the school. The same functions, on behalf of any departmental office in the central administration, can be performed by designated people in those departments.

The concept is really simple. You've probably belonged to a club that elected a publicity chair or designated the corresponding secretary to get notices about meetings to the local paper. Same idea, but broader in scope, with training, resources, and requirements.

Of course, organizing the overall program for an entire school system is not simple, although within one school it is relatively easy. To ensure good work and maximum effectiveness, several important factors must be present. The remainder of this chapter includes a few pointers about those factors.

## Scope of the Assignment

In general, the work of media liaisons is to spread the good news, not to handle the bad news. Crisis communications will typically be handled by the administrator, perhaps with assistance from central office staffers. You've seen sundials with the inscription "only the sunny hours." That cheerful phrase sums up the publicity tasks of the media liaisons. (For additional discussion, see Chapter 7, "Coordinating School and Central Office Responsibilities.")

Of course, if a crisis occurs, such as a missing student or the arrest of a staff member, the principal may ask the media liaison to meet with reporters and camera crews, once the central administration has been consulted and a general response plan agreed upon. Media liaisons develop personal relationships with editors and reporters and insight into how the news media work; this expertise, which administrators may or may not have, comes in handy when sensitive issues are in the spotlight.

## Selecting a Media Liaison

In general, the principal of the school or the top administrator in a central office department should handpick the media liaison to represent the school or department. One important criterion for selection is that the media liaison and the administrator have, or can establish and maintain, a good working relationship. Other qualifications include the willingness to take on the additional assignment (perhaps without remuneration, at least at first), the respect and trust of colleagues, excellent written and oral communications skills, a well-developed ability to use word processors and the fax machine, and a high level of assertiveness accompanied by gracious manners, persistence, and integrity. In short, Superman or Superwoman will do nicely.

In the selection process, administrators should consider the entire staff. Librarians, guidance counselors, secretaries, classroom teachers—all may have the potential to perform well as media liaisons. Administrators at any level, as a rule, have their priorities elsewhere; their responsibilities often preclude any commitment to the routines of sweeping for news, getting out news releases, and making phone calls to pitch stories to local media representatives.

## Working with the Principal

Assuming the basic working relationship is positive, the administrator and the media liaison must then agree on the process for working together—how news will be gathered from the staff, how and when the administrator will inform the media liaison about events and honors, what approval process the administrator will require for releases and media contacts, and so forth. They will also need to agree on the distribution of the releases and the design of the release form.

The importance of close cooperation between the administrator and the media liaison cannot be overemphasized. If the administrator doesn't inform the media liaison about a major event or honor, the opportunity to spread good news is lost, along with the chance to develop community support. The result is frustration and loss of enthusiasm on the part of the staff, especially the media liaison and any sponsoring teachers, parents, or groups. To do an effective job, the media liaison must regularly receive updates about events, programs, and special promotions from everyone in the school or office—and in advance! Nor can the importance of advance notice be overemphasized. A dynamite school program cannot gain TV coverage after it is over. School performances will not gather a crowd if publicized after they have closed. Of course, even when a media liaison gives advance notice to reporters, it's still a good idea to send a last-minute reminder notice on the fax machine the day of the event. The importance of persistence—the squeaky-wheel syndrome—cannot be overemphasized either. In between the advance notices and the last-minute reminders, successful media liaisons also make personal

phone calls to pitch big stories to reporters and editors they know. To stay on top of things, most media liaisons routinely supply their colleagues—well in advance—with photocopied forms seeking the *who, what, when, where, why,* and *how* of their activities. The process of sweeping for news will yield information to translate into news releases for distribution to local media. At this point, the media liaison will be looking for a "news hook"—the appeal, the slant, the unusual aspect of the school activity that will get reporters and camera crews to the school. Remember, the "same old, same old" is not news; it's what's different that's news. So media liaisons have to find out what's different about this year's spelling bee, fun fair, senior play, or recycling program if they want coverage.

Sweeping for news, experienced media liaisons often add a space on their news-gathering forms for staff members to indicate the importance of the activity to the aims of education. The school year is full of promotions such as reading month, math-a-thons, science fairs, spelling bees, field days, musicals and plays, athletics, and more. These events all connect directly to teaching and learning. If the school wants publicity for Career Day, for example, educators cannot leave it to the reporter to connect Career Day with the production of literate citizens and productive workers for the nation. A savvy media liaison and administrator will make the connection explicit, in a way that will increase public support for education in a "big-picture" sense, as well as create publicity for the local school.

Media liaisons will need close working relationships with the PTA, PTO, or PTSA—groups that often take responsibility for school newsletters. Thus, there is a natural overlap between the media liaison's communications effort and the parent organization's effort. Parents are an important audience for school news and, as such, may feel much ownership for the communications efforts of the parent organization. Working cooperatively can decrease the potential territorial squabbles and turf problems that may occur as a result of the natural overlap in functions. However, some parents may not join the PTA/PTO/PTSA and will therefore remain outside the traditional parent communications loop. These parents are still very much a part of the audience for school communications, along with the larger community, and PTA/PTO/PTSA members may be able to help extend communications to reach those who haven't joined the organization.

## Systemwide Coordination and Stipends for the Job

In a large school district with a systemwide media liaison program, one of the communications staff will need to coordinate or manage the program. These duties will include maintaining the roster of media liaisons from each school or office, keeping files of their work, scheduling and planning their training, and providing ongoing assistance and encouragement. It is important, as well, that the media liaisons know they have an advocate at the central office, someone who understands their role and can help them no matter what the situation.

After a media liaison program has been in operation for a year or more, if budgets permit, the coordinator or the superintendent should begin to budget stipends for this extra duty. The media liaison role is similar to that of the partnership coordinator or an after-school coach; it's very important in school and community relations, and thus it merits the recognition of extra work and expertise with a few dollars added to the paycheck. Once remuneration is available, the central administrator also takes the lead in budgeting for the supplemental pay and completing the necessary paperwork so that the media liaisons receive their pay supplements on time. Where budget concerns do not permit extra pay, recertification points to continue licensure are usually welcome.

## Training Media Liaisons

Once the media liaisons are selected, the next step is to plan their training sessions. During these sessions, the coordinator in charge or the designated administrator orients them to their role, walks through a variety of scenarios to illustrate their work, introduces them to news media representatives, and gives hands-on training in the basic tasks, such as writing news releases and pitching a story.

Meeting and hearing from reporters and editors is a key feature of the training sessions. Getting to know each other is basic to good news coverage, and it's instructive to the media liaisons to hear directly from the news media representatives. When a favorite reporter explains her insider views, the media liaisons can learn how to deal directly with those preferences and use them to develop an effective working relationship.

The sessions also should provide basic information about how crisis communications will be handled, so that the media liaisons are clued in, even though they may not have direct responsibilities for the task. It is helpful to suggest that they may volunteer to write a news release or a letter to parents, in case the principal requests such assistance.

When appropriate, media liaisons can help to promote the concept that every school should have its own public relations or communications plan. They can offer their assistance in designing the plan for their respective schools, providing expertise and experience to school administrators.

## A Handbook of Resources

Before the training sessions, the coordinator should prepare a handbook of resources, which becomes the mainstay of the sessions and a reference book for the media liaisons. Sections may include the following:

• Lists of news media contacts in all local media outlets, with mailing addresses, phone numbers, fax numbers, and e-mail addresses.

• A job description of the duties of the media liaison.

• Suggested forms for news releases and for news gathering or sweeping the school for news.

• Selected reference materials, such as sample news releases, pertinent articles from public relations associations, professional associations, and the like.

• Sample parent permission slips to use when students are invited to appear on camera.

• An overview of the program, with rationale and encouraging words about its importance.

• Any applicable school board policies and regulations.

• A letter of appreciation from the superintendent for the media liaison's work.

• The central office coordinator's work phone number, home phone number, fax number, and e-mail address.

## Expecting Performance: Accountability

From the beginning, media liaisons should be asked to submit photocopies of their work and to track their successes as they appear in print and on TV. Copies of their releases enable the coordinator or principal to see how well they have absorbed their training and where they need feedback and encouragement. For example, it may take much practice for them to put the *who, what, when, where, why,* and *how* facts into their releases. Or they may need continuing encouragement to go back to their colleagues to get sufficient detail—not too much, not too little. It takes time to learn that if the basics are lacking, editors won't have a good item to print in local papers. And if releases always come out *after* an event, or lack sufficient phone numbers for easy communication, the TV channels will have no way to cover the event.

Tracking results is time consuming for the media liaisons but important for accountability purposes. It need not be a burden, but a simple matter of clipping stories about their school in local papers and compiling a list of TV and radio appearances. Standards for output can be established, so that media liaisons know from the beginning that their folders in the coordinator's or principal's office must reflect an agreed-upon level of output in order for the stipend to be included in the media liaison's paycheck. Standards should reflect the number of media outlets available in the community, the number of schools competing for the limited space, and the size of the school.

End-of-the-year evaluation conferences are a strong component of performance accountability measures. The media liaison, school (or department) administrator, and the central office administrator in charge of the media liaison program should schedule a meeting. That meeting may cover any matters they wish to discuss, focusing on the performance of the media liaison, the effectiveness of sweeping for news, the number of releases distributed, the clippings file of the media liaison, and the working relationship between the

administrator and the media liaison. Elements of the overall program also come under scrutiny: the training sessions, support from central office, relationships with the news media, the accountability requirements, and the like. Then the central office administrator in charge of the program can incorporate this feedback into improvement of the overall program.

Another end-of-the-year strategy is to send the liaisons a simple questionnaire, with items asking what made the role difficult, what conditions would be ideal for the role, how they informed others in their buildings about their role, what suggestions they have for improvement, and whether they would be willing to take on the responsibility for the next school year. The liaisons' responses can then be used to reshape and improve the program, with ample credit given to the respondents' ideas so that they know their suggestions are appreciated.

## Ongoing Support for Media Liaisons

The central office coordinator should be easily accessible by phone so that media liaisons can ask specific questions as they arise. The coordinator can offer as much individual coaching as necessary or as time permits. Because it is often difficult to make calls on a busy school phone or to get calls returned promptly by those whose primary task is teaching, an especially effective strategy is to send handwritten notes back to the media liaisons to acknowledge and compliment their releases, photos, and tracking records. For instant expressions of appreciation, send notes on the fax machine. Recognition of the work of media liaisons—for example, through photo credits and story credits in employee newsletters—is always a good strategy. Indeed, a systemwide event such as a reception or ceremony in their honor, with the superintendent and school board members thanking them publicly, is a terrific way to express appreciation for their diligent and dedicated work on behalf of school communications.

## How to Create a Media Liaison Program for Your School

Perhaps your work situation doesn't allow the option of working within a centralized media liaison program. You can still adapt the idea to your own school. If you're a faculty or staff member, discuss the possibilities with your principal, and volunteer for the task. If you're a principal, discuss the possibilities at a faculty meeting, and call for a volunteer or request applications if there is agreement that the idea seems worth trying. Once a person has agreed to try the role, here are the basics:

1. Collect the pertinent materials listed in the contents of the handbook of resources, especially the list of news media contacts. Remember the importance of fax numbers for the speedy distribution of news releases. Design appropriate forms on the computer for formatting the releases and for "sweeping" for news; set up a simple numbering system (usually 1-xxx) for releases. Parent permission slips can wait until they are needed for specific TV coverage; a field trip permission slip can be adapted for this purpose.

2. Set up a simple filing system to keep up with copies of releases and clippings to demonstrate the results; include video clips as they become available. Be prepared to tally the results and to explain the program.

3. Learn all you can about the crisis communications plan, just in case the principal needs assistance during a crisis, which can always happen tomorrow.

4. Arrange to meet and talk with local reporters and editors. Find out what their needs are, and explain the role of the media liaison. Work on keeping relationships friendly, and stay in touch with all news media representatives.

5. Refer to Appendix C, "How to Write a News Release," and study the examples given. Refer also to Appendix I, "Media Relations at a Glance," for additional pointers on working with news media representatives.

6. Refer to this chapter for additional ideas about making the program effective, and fine-tune it as you go. Pay particular attention to the development of positive and supportive relationships with faculty and staff and with parent groups.

7. Remember to send copies of news releases to community and civic groups, as well as to locally elected officials. Just be sure each release is letter-perfect in spelling and usage—embarrassing errors will tarnish the school's image.

# 7

# Coordinating School
# and Central Office Responsibilities

You will find that life is a game, sometimes serious, sometimes fun,
but a game that must be played with true team-spirit.
—SHELAGH DELANEY, MODERN BRITISH PLAYWRIGHT

Principals and central office administrators often discuss the issues and delineate the various functions in personnel decisions, budgeting, and curriculum, especially when moving to site-based management or adjusting to administrative reorganizations. After all, people at all levels of the organization need a clear, shared view of how to work together. Similarly, they must make decisions about who handles what aspect of communications. Issues of territory and prerogatives are bound to arise among all who have responsibilities for the news.

At first, in a decentralizing or downsizing school system, principals may be expected to manage all school-based news and events, simply adding this responsibility to their job descriptions. This sounds simple but, in action,

raises questions. Who handles the media, for example, if asbestos contamination is found within a school—the principal, the media liaison, the superintendent, the assistant superintendent for facilities, or the central office communications staff? And who handles questions from concerned parents? Similarly, who distributes the news release when a team wins a state championship—is it a school story or a systemwide story? Who puts the announcement in the paper when the school board schedules a public forum in a high school auditorium—the clerk of the board or the media liaison for the school?

Sooner or later, such questions require thoughtful discussion so that everyone can "sing from the same page" and therefore handle any situation calmly and smoothly. Remember: your ability to coordinate sensitive or difficult situations can make or break the image of your school and system in the news. (See also Figure 7.1.)

Circumstances will vary from system to system and from school to school, but a few guiding principles can assist you in making careful decisions about procedures, no matter how large or small, how rural or urban the district. Here are guidelines for five types of situations: (1) when school news is bad news, (2) when school news is major good news, (3) when a school story has systemwide importance, (4) when system initiatives take place at one school or a few—pilot programs, and (5) when

## Figure 7.1.
## Whose Story Is It?

| Responsibility | School<br>Principal<br>and Media Liaison | Central Office<br>Superintendent<br>and Central Office Staff |
| --- | --- | --- |
| Good news | meetings<br>announcements<br>special events<br>contests<br>promotions<br>within-school awards<br>academic accomplishments<br>sports<br>features<br>parenting workshops<br>partnership activities | major awards<br>new buildings<br>achievement data<br>special events<br>meetings<br>systemwide promotions |
| Bad news | | weather emergencies<br>vandalism, crimes, arrests<br>accidents, illnesses<br>fires, explosions, floods<br>violence, deaths, tragedies<br>environmental hazards |
| General | | school board actions<br>exemplary practices<br>promising innovations<br>important guests<br>day-to-day business<br>systemwide public meetings<br>budget matters<br>policies and regulations |

the release of systemwide data causes fallout on schools. You can adjust these guidelines to suit your own school and system.

## When School News Is Bad News

In making the decision about whose story it is, the good news/bad news dimension is the first principle to consider. The rule of thumb, as mentioned in the discussion about the responsibilities of media liaisons, is that the school takes care of good news and central office staff must manage bad news. Bad news may include the arrest of an employee, charges against an administrator or a teacher, environmental hazards, violence, fire or explosion, vandalism, break-ins, and the like.

Any bad news emanating from any school almost certainly causes negative fallout on the entire system. Negative fallout can include political outcomes, financial questions, legal implications, tarnished image, and loss of public confidence. These far-reaching consequences must be addressed by the upper-level administrators, the superintendent, and the school board; that's why the central office staff must take the primary role in handling bad news. However, at the same time, the school staff have important roles to play in the effort. In a crisis at any specific school, the principal will have the legal responsibility for the operation of the school, as well as insights into and familiarity with the community. So responding to bad news requires teamwork between the

central office and the school, although the central office takes the lead.

The first step in ensuring teamwork is to establish some kind of "early warning system" so that the principal notifies the appropriate person at central office as soon as a crisis occurs. The early warning system sets the mechanisms for response in motion as quickly as possible. Normally, such a system should include both "heads-up" phone calls and fax reports with details. It's important to maintain a record of how quickly contacts are made and appropriate responses initiated.

To illustrate the teamwork, here's an example. In an old wing of an elementary school, a chunk of the ceiling in a teachers' closet suddenly gave way, leaving cabinets and supplies coated with dust. Fortunately, no one was hurt, but environmental engineers found asbestos particles in the dust. The principal had to move the class out of the adjacent classroom immediately, notify all families about the danger, make interim plans for housing classes and then notify them about the plans, and arrange for the cleanup.

His first step, when the report came in from the environmental engineer's office, was to notify the superintendent's office—this was the early warning to central office. Next, the principal requested assistance from the central office communications staff. He called a schoolwide parents' meeting to ensure face-to-face communication about the crisis; for the meeting, he received assistance from the central office staff in preparing a fact sheet to duplicate and distribute. At the same time, he received suggestions about how to respond to the media, who soon called for on-camera interviews. Occasionally, as the crisis was resolved, the system's official spokesperson also appeared on camera on behalf of the principal.

During the entire time this school was in the news, close communication and cooperation, back and forth between the school and the central office, enabled the principal to approach parents and the larger community in a well-organized manner, which supported a positive image of the school, despite the crisis. This professional conduct reflected well on the superintendent and the school board, who did not have to appear on camera but who did visit the school during the crisis.

## When School News Is Major Good News

When the news is good, there's no crisis, but the teamwork operates the same way. You can communicate unusual or major good news to central office as soon as it happens. You want to keep the central administration and the school board informed about important events, such as major awards, the visit of a state or federal policymaker, new degrees or significant honors bestowed upon students or employees, and the like. Such important good news may be worthy of recognition at a school board meeting, a letter of congratulations from the superintendent, inclusion in systemwide

newsletters, or a special push for media coverage— that is, both from the media liaison or principal and from the central communications staff.

For example, when a high school teacher was named "state foreign language teacher of the year," the principal and the media liaison called the central office staff, who then wrote and distributed the news release, pitched the story to newspaper and TV reporters, and included an announcement in the employee newsletter. Similarly, a middle school principal was named "state principal of the year," and the same kind of teamwork prevailed, yielding TV coverage just as he returned from a trip, with a crowd of well-wishers greeting him, complete with a huge banner and the school cheerleaders—great visuals!

In another example, a cafeteria worker at an elementary school saved the life of a choking student by using the Heimlich maneuver. As you might expect, this story immediately received media coverage with little encouragement from the school. Later, however, the central office communications staff arranged a special school board recognition for the food service employee.

One more example: An elementary cafeteria won an award from the U.S. Department of Agriculture for providing excellent food service for children with disabilities. The central office staff arranged for filming by the community cable TV channel of the award presentation, followed by a later cable news story detailing that cafeteria's preparation of food for children with special needs. Schools are full of wonderful news stories like these, and teamwork between school and central office helps to ensure that the good news receives the best possible coverage.

## When a School Story Has Systemwide Importance

In deciding who handles a story, it's important to consider the occasions when an individual school symbolically represents the entire system. These are occasions when the school as an entity is recognized for special achievements, such as the Parents' Magazine Awards, Blue Ribbon School designations, Inviting School Awards, state and national competitions, program certifications, and the like. In these cases, the system feels some ownership and should reflect some of the glory surrounding the school, even though the occasion is actually the province of the school itself.

Naturally, efforts to publicize these positive stories should reflect cooperation between the school and the central office. Central office staff can assist principals and media liaisons in getting pertinent quotations from the superintendent and school board members for the school's news release, pitching the story to the news media, arranging school board recognitions, and scheduling on-camera interviews with upper-level administrators and school board members.

A school occasion of special systemwide importance is the dedication of a new school building or an addition or the reopening of a renovated building. Because the capital outlay budget represents a major commitment from the taxpayers of the community, a new or renovated facility is a matter of interest in the entire community. The celebration surrounding a new building will necessarily call for the participation of policymakers who budgeted the dollars and for teamwork to spread the news throughout the community. Shining an appreciative spotlight on the elected officials responsible for the new facility is an opportunity for communicating with them under the best of circumstances and creating supportive relationships for the future. A dedication provides them the chance to interact with their constituents in a very favorable light.

To dedicate a new middle school, for example, the principal knew he should invite the school board, the city council, and all other locally elected officials to the ceremony. And, on such a special occasion, it was also important to involve all employees and to include students and parents as well as the business partners of the school. The principal appointed a planning committee headed by an assistant principal. When the committee began to make plans, many questions and concerns about protocol and politics popped up. How should the seats on the stage be allocated, and to whom? Who should be seated by whom? Would there be room for the chorus and the VIPs on the stage at the same time? Which VIPs should receive official introduction? Who should do the official welcome? How could every student be included? Could the teachers and students serve as hosts and hostesses for the tour of the school? What about the classified employees? Which should come first—the tour, the ceremony, or the refreshments? The assistant principal, who had not encountered this situation before, called upon the central office staff for help because they had assisted with several dedications in the past. Together, the central office staff and the planning committee worked out the details, serving the interests of both the school and the system through two-way cooperation and communication.

A side note here: The preparation of a printed program or brochure about the new facility is often undertaken by the architectural or engineering firm guiding the project, at no cost to the school or system, specifically for use at the dedication. Such materials, however, serve primarily as marketing materials for the firm, not for the school. Fortunately, such firms are usually open to input from the school and willing to work with the principal or other staff in the preparation of materials. This means you have a terrific opportunity to see that the materials carry school messages as well as messages from the firm.

You can emphasize such themes as how the new facility will serve the needs of instructional programs, expand the library/media center, create a sense of community among students, provide new technologies to students and teachers, incorporate design ideas and decor from many cultures, and help to serve the community's needs for facilities,

too—whatever is true in the case of your new facility. You can also check the firm's method of handling the information about the costs of construction and planning. Building costs should be honestly explained and broken down in ways that make sense to the public.

Because costs can be a hot button to many people in the community, you need to discuss the best way to present the information with the people at the firm who are preparing the material. You should consider comparing the square-footage costs of the new facility with the average square-footage costs in your state or system. You may also consider comparing average square-footage costs over time in your state to provide some perspective on how these have changed. Last, you may want to provide a bulleted list of the features in the facility made possible by the square-footage costs, alongside a similar list of features from a facility built 50 years ago, with the average square-footage costs of 50 years ago or for a time frame for which you can locate the comparable data. There's no getting around increases in building costs over the years; the important thing is to present the information so that the public can see the value of what it is getting in return for its tax contributions.

## When System Initiatives Take Place at One School or a Few— Pilot Programs

Certain system initiatives also require close cooperation between the system and the school, whether they stem from efforts of the school board, the superintendent, or the instructional staff. Such initiatives as pilots for new instructional programs, school reform programs, the implementation of state standards, the field testing of programs or assessments, the trial of a peer mediation program, acceptance by the International Baccalaureate program—these usually take place at one school or a few, but the implication is that they may spread throughout the system if they prove effective. Sometimes, program initiatives are addressed to schools with particular characteristics, such as when the system contracts with several providers for services to, say, Title I schools or schools failing to meet state standards. For example, perhaps the system is addressing low achievement by offering low-performing schools several models of improvement, such as Accelerated Schools, the Comer School Development Program, and Success for All. The responsibility for such stories most often resides with the central office communications staff, who will require the assistance of the principal, teachers, and media liaison in the school in handling the story over the school year or longer.

## When the Release of Systemwide Data Causes Fallout on Schools

In today's world of accountability, test score data and other school profile information, such as pupil-teacher ratios, per pupil expenditures, faculty qualifications, and racial and ethnic data, are usually released by the system or the state. The school usually has no choice about the release date and no influence on the publication of such data, which are most often ranked by school within each system. Indeed, the system has no choice and no influence over when the information is released by the state. Yet the release of such data may cause negative fallout.

In advance of the release by the system or the state, an individual school or the system should prepare its own news release about its performance or profile. Then the principal or media liaison or central office staffer can issue this news release as soon as is practical after the release of the perhaps disturbing data. From either perspective, pertinent explanations of test score levels—whether they are high or low or in the middle—should be noted; any aberrations in testing should be incorporated into interpretations without, however, making the interpretations sound like apologies or excuses. In other words, the strengths and weaknesses at the school or in the system should be addressed straightforwardly and honestly, no matter whether the school or system is considered high-performing, low-performing, or in between. For a response from the system, the central office staff will need to prepare a news release separate from those prepared by the schools, with the interpretations and explanations needed from the central office perspective.

From either perspective, it is especially helpful to maintain records of data over time, so that you can report trends in student achievement or faculty qualifications or racial and ethnic composition—whatever the hot topics may be at the moment. To accompany test score data, you can briefly mention school or system initiatives that may lead to better achievement in the future. Or you can use the occasion to make a request to the community for volunteer tutors to assist students in improving their learning. These kinds of responses work equally well in on-camera interviews.

It is also a good idea to keep data on topics that balance the reporting and ranking of test score data, such as scholarships earned by seniors, the percentage of graduates entering post-secondary education, numbers of students enrolled in Advanced Placement courses, dropout rates, mobility rates, disciplinary incidents, number of students qualifying for the honor roll, library book circulation, number of computers, and the like. Then, in a "down" year when test scores decline, you will have data to show how your school has improved in another important area of public and parental concern.

If you appear in on-camera interviews, these examples should be just as effective as they are in news releases.

## Benefits of Coordinating School and Central Office Responses

The foregoing discussion illustrates a few guiding principles that you may use as presented here or as a starting point for further discussions. You may also refer to Chapters 6 and 8 for other ideas. As a team, you and your colleagues can suggest and evaluate procedures for handling each kind of story, ironing out differences of opinion and coming to consensus about the most effective ways to manage the news. Then you can work out your own approach based on your circumstances. What you are hoping for, in the long run, is smooth operation in managing the news, without territorial battles, so that your school and your system maintain a positive image even during a crisis, simply because you managed the news professionally and knowledgeably.

# Communications from the Central Office Perspective

Teachers and principals with expertise in writing or community relations often find themselves serving as communications officers or public relations staffers in the central offices of school systems. It's an exciting opportunity for anyone, and a real challenge for those without professional certification in the field of public relations. Still, as this book has suggested, communications is just a special kind of teaching, and your instincts for sending varied messages to varied audiences are likely to be right on target. This chapter presents an overview of some aspects of the central office perspective.

In a central office communications role, your scope is likely to be broader and more complex than in a school—broader because you must juggle the needs of schools with the needs of central office, more complex because the political implications of your work may be far-reaching. In central office, your top priority must necessarily be serving the superintendent, other upper-level administrators and their departments, and the school board. They are likely to request services not needed at a school, such as writing speeches and board meeting summaries, organizing news conferences and community forums, providing photographs and résumés, conducting public opinion surveys, and the like. The following sections address a few of the particular concerns of central office staffers.

## The "No Surprises" Rule

Top administrators and school board members leading school systems in today's politically charged environments must remain on high alert. They must scrutinize every development, large or small, for its political ramifications. In this climate, and especially because you will be working with the news media, you must strive for "no surprises" in all your dealings with the leaders. This means notifying them about news media inquiries, stories scheduled to run on TV or in the paper, concerns of patrons—anything and everything you hear that could lead to concern or comment. It also means ensuring appropriate review, before publishing any material about any facet of the operation of the system, by the administrator in charge. You need to build in these assurances in the form of routine procedures and to practice them daily.

Insofar as possible, alert your administrators about emerging issues before they attend meetings in the community or receive phone calls from alarmed patrons. In meetings or conversations, they don't want to come across as ignorant; they want to be prepared.

Part of the "no surprises" strategy is to ensure that the preferences of the top administrators regarding the release of information are followed to the letter. You should find some helpful suggestions for reaching agreement on the release of information in the following discussion on "Getting Started: Hard News." You should also find the section on "Issues Management: Scoping Out the Territory Ahead" useful for concepts regarding the intake or listening side of communication.

## Dealing with Time Constraints

The upper-echelon leaders are perennially short on time. Pulled in every direction, they have little time to devote to back-and-forth reviews, even when giving heartfelt support to your efforts. Don't let this become a problem. Just cultivate the ability to sense opinions, preferences, and developments, and the confidence to select the best course of action when it's not at all clear.

When you are beginning, if you experience delays in getting reviews, try being creative, such as catching an administrator in the parking lot or hallway for a quick look at a news release. It helps to know who arrives early and who works late, so that you have a good chance of finding an administrator on the day you need to get a review or specific information for completing a task. The secretaries can also assist you in getting these essential tasks accomplished, so establish good working relationships throughout the office, and do your best to work as part of a team.

Count yourself lucky if you receive prompt replies to your questions. Promptness will give you quick turnarounds, enabling you to get direction and feedback and thus protecting everyone from those dreaded surprises you are trying to avoid. Only when a lengthy face-to-face conversation is needed will you have to schedule a sit-down appointment. Be polite but persistent in getting feedback and approval as quickly as possible. You don't want busy schedules to crowd out the exchange of information or the approval of work; you're trying to uphold the "no surprises" rule. Inevitably there will be times when you will have to do the best you can with limited feedback and review. It's part of the job.

## Getting Started: Hard News

Many top-level administrators have handled media relations and crisis communications more or less on their own for much of their careers, especially in small school districts. Until employed by a large district, they may not have worked with a media spokesperson, let alone with a full-fledged communications program. As a result, they may not be accustomed to delegating the tasks of managing "hard news." But what if it's your first day on the job and your first call tells you that a body has been discovered behind a portable classroom by drivers education students arriving early in the morning for class? You must be prepared to handle such a call.

There's no substitute for coming to agreement as soon as possible with top-level administrators as to just how your work will proceed, even before you are officially on the job. This means, first, identifying the services you can provide and then discussing them openly with those you serve. You will thus get to know their preferences and concerns, and you can explain what you will need from them. In the absence of a crisis during your first week on the job, begin by discussing emergency closing (or inclement weather) procedures, because they are usually familiar and easy to accept.

Once you've agreed on those, you can address the management of other crises or hard news situations, using emergency closings procedures as a model to guide the discussion. (Also refer to Chapter 7 for suggestions about coordinating central office and school responses to crises.) Then you can move forward with discussions about executive services, baseline communications, and "soft news," though usually not all at once. And you can let the top administrators know that you'll soon be asking for feedback on a communications plan for the system. When they review the plan, you'll have another occasion for developing common understandings about the scope and direction of your work.

Eventually, your colleagues will see the positive results of your assistance in managing hard news. They will appreciate the benefits, for example, of having a spokesperson who takes the on-camera role during a crisis or of having fact sheets prepared to give complete information to parents and the public during the aftermath of a school fire, a conflict about rezoning, or a violent incident. Over time, working together should establish credibility and trust.

## Access to Information: Controlled? Open?

Top-level administrators and school board members know full well that "information is power." Much of their effectiveness on the job stems from their knowledge of private and confidential information. Constantly trying to resolve sensitive political, personnel, and financial matters, they may be wary of open access to information. And they may have private, unspoken concerns about the public's right to know, despite their knowledge of, and adherence to, legal requirements such as sunshine laws and freedom-of-information laws. From their point of view, they are being prudent in guarding the release of sensitive information and in being wary of the news business. Therefore, they may exert firm control over the release of information of any sort.

Such firm control may be expressed in extensive requirements for review and approval of documents and data within each department and then by the superintendent. If each administrator in the chain of command has authority for review and approval, "leaks" will be minimized and control of information assured—at least that's the intent. Occasionally, a top administrator will expect to exercise review and approval prerogatives unilaterally.

You can take the lead in preparing guidelines about access to and release of information for review by top-level administrators, or you can follow their direction or the direction of the superintendent. It is essential to reassure

administrators that you will not release stories, news releases, or material of any sort that they have not reviewed and approved when the information relates to their departments. And you must take the lead in managing Freedom of Information Act (FOIA) requests, which must be communicated consistently to staff and media representatives and then followed faithfully. Periodic conversations to review how the guidelines are working are helpful in determining whether procedures need to be adjusted, so that comfort levels and confidence in your work are maintained.

Top-level administrators who are extremely cautious about access to information usually exhibit enthusiasm for the "good news" or "publicity" side of communications. As a rule, you will find them receptive to your efforts to show the school system at its best, highlighting awards and recognitions, accomplishments and achievements. Success in getting "good ink" will be well received and will make the difficulties inherent in your job easier in the long run.

## Issues Management: Scoping Out the Territory Ahead

*Issues management* (or *issue management*) is an unfamiliar term for a familiar process, that of "taking the pulse" of the community, or of one's constituents. Essentially, issues management is made possible when communications programs emphasize *listening* to people as well as *sending messages* to varied audiences. A one-way communications effort sends news out; a two-way communications effort also brings news in.

As tidbits of news come in, you can discern what is on the minds of people, look for patterns of opinions, and then develop a strategy for how best to handle concerns before they become inflammatory. Issues management is like sending scouts out ahead of the wagon train—you need a way of scoping out the territory ahead, predicting trouble, and altering your course if there's danger in your path.

Naturally top-level administrators and the school board are interested in anticipating strong sentiments, predicting any conflicts and controversies about to erupt, and preparing to solve emerging problems before they get out of hand. That's why it's important to find out what's on the minds of employees and people in the community. Part of your work, therefore, is the listening end of communication. After identifying potential issues, you will also be able to recommend ways to avoid difficulties, strategies for handling them, or suggestions for altering existing strategies to take the new issues into account.

Typically, top-level administrators practice issues management by intuition. After all, they are privy to confidential information from within the organization and from the community—an endless stream of rumor, gossip, hearsay, and innuendo from the grapevine. All these formal and informal sources contribute to their continuous efforts to anticipate emerging issues within the organization and the community, to "stay on top of things."

As part of your issues management approach, you can design focus groups to solicit from the members of any constituency their ideas about what issues or needs or topics or conflicts are on the minds of people in that particular group. It's like conducting an in-person survey of emerging issues (see Appendix J).

You'll find issues management an important part of strategic thinking about public relations, that is, the problem-solving aspects. "Keeping your ear to the ground," you will often hear concerns before anyone else does; you can pass these along to the appropriate administrators, and especially to the superintendent. Certainly it is helpful for you to share the results of any surveys, interviews, hot lines, complaints, focus groups, and the like. Thus, you may be able to contribute substantively to the administrators' awareness by informing them of potential issues as you hear about them. In your own work, you can use the information to shape messages sensitively before they go out to the community and to employees. You can eventually illustrate your own issues management approach for presentation to the administrators to portray your views of how the process works and seek their feedback for improvements.

## Executive Services

Upper-echelon administrators and school board members usually welcome assistance in such executive services as correspondence, speech writing, special events, résumé management, and the maintenance of stock photo files. Offering these services is a good idea, because the needs are keenly felt and comfort levels are high. Fortunately, the leaders are also familiar with the process of drafting, correcting, rewriting, reviewing again, and so on. This familiar process can serve as a good example when you explain other review and approval processes and the give-and-take nature of work in communications. Included here are a few specific suggestions for these popular executive services.

## Correspondence

Top-level administrators and school board members are accustomed to assistance with correspondence, because the volume of letters they receive can be overwhelming and failure to respond promptly can become a damaging political issue. Many secretaries supply such services very well, and your assistance should supplement or complement their established support. However, to streamline the process, you may suggest the use of a handbook of form letters for the predictable kinds of responses that recur often. You may locate such a handbook from a commercial publisher or develop your own by classifying the types of letters in the files and then developing your own forms for a mail-merge system. Just don't forget there will always be a need for individually written responses to particular concerns; these require the personal touch.

Be aware also that various staff members may possess professional expertise on matters of concern to the letter writers. For example, to answer a letter expressing serious concern about a curriculum issue, you should consult appropriate staff in the curriculum department. Or to respond to a complaint about a specific textbook, you may have to find out the details of the textbook selection process from the person in charge. Make it a practice to consult your colleagues so that your replies are accurate and informative.

For the top-level administrators, consider recommending that they use personalized official stationery for writing brief personal handwritten notes of recognition and appreciation. Be prepared to manage the design and printing of such stationery with the district's logo, motto, and so forth. Such personal notes are a great boon to the image of the leaders.

E-mail correspondence is rapidly replacing some types of letters and memos. Your office may or may not be one where standard interoffice memos, for example, have become an endangered species. Still, the management of e-mail correspondence is worth examining. Most e-mail is managed by the individual administrators themselves; however, you can suggest that certain requests and complaints from the public be forwarded to your office or to the office of appropriate staff members for responses. If so, be sure to clarify how copies will be preserved and files maintained for the record, so that no information is lost.

You will need special help in preparing correspondence for state legislators, governors, members of Congress, and other officials and dignitaries. Be sure to collect and consult appropriate guides on executive manners and then to follow the recommended protocols for correct form. The communications staff in your state department of education may be able to suggest specific sources appropriate for your state. Be very sensitive to these fine points, and the image of the school system will be enhanced.

## Speech Writing

Speech writing is well accepted as an executive service. In approaching the task, it's ideal to confer with the person requesting the speech so that you know in advance the sentiments he or she would like to express on the occasion in question. You can then ask whether the person prefers a complete draft, an outline of points or topics with bulleted items, or some format between the two. You can inquire about preferred type size and line length and arrangement for the final print-out. The administrator or board member might contribute information about the inviting organization, points, anecdotes, phrases, or other ideas for incorporation into the speech and likely would appreciate suggestions from you as well. Then you would compose a first draft, submit that for correction and feedback, and revise it until it gained full approval in its complete form.

Ideally, too, you would listen while the administrator practices delivery of the speech. Then you would offer suggestions to improve

delivery. Practicing in front of a small but encouraging audience is very helpful in refining a speech, so recruit a few colleagues to listen, too. This enables your client and you to tackle questions of dramatic emphasis, appropriate gestures, pronunciation and accent, fluctuations in voice volume, and effective use of microphones and sound systems, for example.

Plan to provide the final copy of the speech in a three-ring binder, printed in the format preferred by the administrator. In general, speeches should be printed in 14- to 18-point type, triple spaced, perhaps boldface to stand out. Avoid right-justified margins, and shorten the line length so that the left-justified lines are easy to take in with one sweep of the eyes. Also, in general, typefaces that resemble traditional textbook print—that is, serif type—are easier to read than sans serif styles. Avoid the use of all capital letters, unless your client prefers that style. Include any advance information in the pockets of the binder, such as programs, lists of dignitaries, officers of the organization. Because busy people need reminders, be sure the date, time, and place are conveniently available—perhaps printed right on the cover insert, along with the administrator's name. And to cover all eventualities, ask a colleague who will attend the same meeting to take an extra copy of the speech along, just in case the official copy is mislaid somewhere along the way.

Occasionally, for a very important speech, you may prepare advance copies for the news media. If you decide to do this, request assistance in advance from colleagues who are skilled in proofreading. Absolute correctness and accuracy in every respect must be ensured. Under no circumstances should you let copies be distributed with careless errors still in them. The resulting damage to the system's image would not be easily undone.

Finally, file the speech in your own file. Eventually you will accumulate speeches of several lengths for different occasions. Keep any discarded notes that may be useful for later speeches. Be sure to keep your records clear about when and where each was delivered—no one wants to give similar speeches to the same group, not even years apart.

Realistically, things aren't always ideal, and you may find yourself drafting a speech in a hurry, with very little time and information. You may know only the occasion and the type of speech desired (welcome, greetings, remarks, or speeches of varying durations). Further, you may suddenly be asked to prepare two speeches for different groups during the same time frame. Your client colleague may not even be available to describe the sentiments to be expressed in the speech. In other words, you are on your own, and there's not much time.

Perhaps you have in the files a similar speech used for a similar occasion—something you can adapt quickly. You may find it necessary to talk with the contact person in the organization extending the invitation, so that you can gain more background information about the occasion, the organization, and the reason for the invitation. After you quickly

gather all the information you can, your role as ghostwriter is very much a matter of creativity and imagination, familiarity with the values and positions of the person requesting the speech, familiarity with issues in the community or the inviting organization, and expertise in the field of education.

To check your work, read the first draft aloud to yourself as you go, listening for rough spots and timing your own delivery. Correct the speech to please your own ear, and print it out in the preferred style, or in shortened, left-justified phrases in 14- to 18-point type for easy scanning from the podium. If you find you have time only to draft the speech and hand it to your colleague as he or she departs for the occasion, just say "good luck" and hope for the best.

You will need a few reference books or online Web sites to assist you in composing speeches, whether you are writing under ideal or less-than-ideal circumstances. Look for books of quotations, collections of jokes and anecdotes compiled for the purpose, and poetry anthologies; and make sure that anything you use is not offensive to anyone. Be sure your reference collection reflects a variety of ethnic groups and cultures, patriotic and historic sources, and expert views on education issues. If you happen to have a dated book of quotations, for example, keep it as a source but supplement it with newer and culturally diverse sources, so that administrators can communicate effectively with today's audiences.

## Computer-Assisted and Multimedia Presentations

For all services that are variations on speech writing, top-level administrators and board members usually require skilled editorial and technical assistance, and they are typically happy to have such help. Scripting a multimedia presentation is very similar to the production of an information video, requiring highly skilled people to manage the integration of the media into a cohesive whole. The use of computer-assisted presentations depends heavily on the available software and the skill of the person generating the computer graphics. If you possess any or all of these skills, your clients are lucky indeed. If you do not, you may want to begin identifying employees or vendors who can assist when you need them.

## Special Events

Another public relations arena where top administrators are comfortable with delegating tasks to staff members is that of special events. Few want to concern themselves with the actual arrangements, although they certainly do want to set the tone, identify major speakers, and review possible settings, themes, and the like. In general, they are familiar with the give-and-take process of orchestrating special events.

The variety of special events organized by school systems is immense, and there are usually informal traditions or customary ways of doing things that have taken hold over the years. If you find yourself unexpectedly given the responsibility for planning a major special event as one of your first assignments—say, for a systemwide back-to-school meeting—you would be wise to consult with all staffers who have contributed to planning the event in years past. Draw on their experiences, and share the tasks of planning and coordination.

You will need reference books to accomplish this planning function, as well as executive etiquette guides. Peruse the sources available in special events or event planning, and collect those that seem most appropriate in your system. Be sensitive to matters of protocol, especially when your event includes elected officials and dignitaries from your community. You can develop your own planning guides, but to do so is time consuming. It may be easier to adapt the commercially produced guides. Even a wedding planner offers some useful ideas if you just adapt them to the events in the school system.

## Stock Photo Files

Those who work in central office usually receive frequent requests for photos of top-level administrators and school board members. To answer such requests readily, you will want to develop or maintain a stock photo file. To ensure that you have photos of all current top-level administrators and school board members available and that they are of equivalent and excellent quality, you can arrange appointments for everyone with well-established commercial photographers. Or, to economize, you may seek the services of any available governmental agency photographers or call in a colleague who has a good reputation and admirable skill as an amateur photographer. Once the proofs are back, be sure to allow each person to select the pose he or she prefers—people are very sensitive about their own public images. Don't be surprised if some have to be redone. And remember, these should be black-and-white photographs, which exhibit superior contrasts suitable for printing.

In addition to portraits or "mug" shots, save informal photos and candid shots throughout the years, whether they are in color or black and white. These will come in handy for future publications or for special requests. Before the collection gets large, decide on appropriate categories and expand the file so that you have photos on hand for most uses. You will always need the option of commissioning specific photo shoots for certain occasions, such as when the superintendent announces the selection of the "teacher of the year" with a surprise visit to the classroom, or the ceremony at which newly elected board members are sworn in.

### Résumé Management

In addition to requests for photos, you are likely to receive numerous requests for one-page vitas for top-level administrators and school board members, to be used as background material for introductions at public appearances. To fulfill these requests, you will need to keep an updated supply of vitas on hand or readily available on the computer.

Occasionally these are changed to meet the needs of a particular occasion; for example, when a top-level administrator addresses a teachers' association, he or she may want to insert additional information about his or her current or previous membership in that association.

You may also maintain full professional résumés in the files and on computer, with periodic reviews and additions to keep them up to date. Full professional résumés may be required to accompany grants applications, professional association program proposals, and submissions to awards competitions. Such résumés should always reflect the best image of the school system and its leaders. If you find that your colleagues' résumés have not been professionally designed and edited, suggest that this would improve the appearance of their résumés, and follow through on securing such assistance.

## Developing Common Understandings Through Training

In-house staff development and training can be very helpful in creating common understandings about communications in general and the specific benefits of a strong program in gaining community support. You may design your own sessions for formal training, and you will undoubtedly be participating in many conversations, meetings, and discussions to explain your work and develop the common understandings. You may also schedule regular sessions with reporters and editors, for example, so that your colleagues can experience the point of view of the media representatives and develop empathy for their efforts and the role of a free press in our society.

Now and then, an outside expert may be the best investment you can make to gain support for your work; the credibility of the outside expert enhances open-mindedness and reduces resistance to new concepts. If so, call in a media consultant for training sessions for school board members, administrators, media liaisons, and teachers. These occasions give you a chance to extend awareness of the realities of communications and to demonstrate the importance of expertise in the field. Media consultants are usually adept at fostering understanding of the many different perspectives in school communications—the attitudes of the public, of employees, of opinion leaders, and so on. It is always comforting to learn that other school systems face situations like your own knottiest communications problems. And it is helpful to learn how other systems address those problems. Such training sessions are also terrific opportunities to participate in a common dialogue with the superintendent and the school board. Learning things together can serve as the basis for working together more effectively within the system and in the schools.

Sometimes a consultant can make points or create awareness of professional strategies that you have not been able to accomplish on your own. When you have a media consultant lined up for a session, confer with that person in the planning stages, indeed, before any contract is signed. Be candid and clear about any situations in the school or system or community, and see how the consultant can incorporate these local issues into his or her presentation. If the vibrations are good, you may also explain certain points that need to be made or reinforced. This subtle, indirect approach may convey your message very effectively to the superintendent, school board members, administrators, and media liaisons.

The training experience, once it is over, becomes a new reference point; you will be able to refer to the lessons learned with everyone who participated. Consider establishing repeat training sessions with the same consultant to give continuity and familiarity to the learning process. The consultant can address different audiences within the system on the same topic as the first session or can present additional topics to the original audience. You'll find several organizations listed in Appendix J that can supply well-qualified consultants. Your state department of education may also have staff members who can fill this role. Local and state members of the Public Relations Society of America may also be available.

## Arranging a News Conference

From time to time, your superintendent or school board may need to make an announcement worthy of broad media attention. A news conference will highlight the importance of the announcement and give the media spotlight to the decision makers. Here are a few suggestions to get you started in making the necessary arrangements:

• Given the nature and timing of the announcement to be made, start the scheduling process with the superintendent and the school board and anyone else directly involved. Then schedule the news conference according to the most convenient time of day for local reporters and editors.

• If the middle of the day turns out to be a convenient time for everyone involved, consider serving a simple box lunch, if the budget permits. Reporters and editors are likely to be stressed for time; giving them lunch is a way of helping them work your news conference into their hectic schedules.

• Determine, in consultation with your superintendent, whether any material will be embargoed for actual release at a later time the same day or at a later date. Assist the superintendent in preparing for the news conference, forecasting possible responses and discussing how the conference will best be managed.

• Send an advance media alert—a very brief special news release—to announce the news conference; provide the date, time, and place, the topic to be announced, and parking arrangements; and give the names of the people who will be involved. It's not necessary to give the details of the story in the advance notice. Distribute these alerts on the fax machine as you would any other news release.

• Consider whether someone will need to emcee the conference or whether the superintendent will handle that function. It may be helpful to have an experienced staff member fill this role, particularly if you expect a large crowd, but most superintendents are quite comfortable both calling on reporters and answering their questions. Plan for this role according to your superintendent's preferences.

• Consider asking a colleague to serve as host or hostess. This person welcomes everyone who arrives, pointing out seating and handing out press packets. You may be able to do this yourself, but you may be very busy taking care of the needs of the superintendent or other dignitaries.

• Prepare press packets for all who will attend the news conference. Press packets usually include a news release, any pertinent background materials (such as a brochure from an architectural firm, a fact sheet about a crisis, or a budget document), 8" X 10" black-and-white photos, notes from students, and so forth. (A note about photos of new or renovated buildings: These photos will be more effective if they show how students and teachers will use the facilities. Many photos supplied by architectural photographers feature the structure itself rather than its human uses; showing the human uses will help taxpayers and citizens see how the building contributes to the education of young people, rather than merely the structure as a design.) If materials are embargoed, include this information in large, boldface type at the top of the release, along with the time and date when the embargo ends. An ordinary file folder will do nicely to contain the assorted materials, but you may also use glossy, colored folders with pockets inside to hold the supplementary materials. You may also attach stickers bearing the school or system logo, include small favors, and insert your card or the superintendent's. You may want to consider having such folders specially printed to keep on hand for this use, if the budget permits.

• The day before, place phone calls to reporters and editors to hint at the importance of the forthcoming announcement and generate interest in the news conference. You may even repeat these calls on the day of the news conference. Be your most persuasive, helpful, and charming self.

• At the appointed hour, welcome all comers to the news conference with greetings at the door and the press packets readily available. Ensure access to phones, if needed, and assist in scheduling later interviews, if requested.

## Cutting the Communications Budget—Don't!

As administrators and school boards struggle with budgets, they are often tempted to cut the budget for the communications program. School systems rarely have enough money to hire public information officers, employ marketing firms, or pay for professional design and editing. Educators' habits of frugality are one reason they have often ignored baseline communications and concentrated on crisis communications.

In setting budget priorities, public relations may be called "fluff." Sometimes one or two complaints about printing or mailing costs will cause a superintendent or school board to determine that the newsletters or brochures are not necessary. Any number of arguments can be advanced, and will be, as to why a school system does not need a Web site, an employee newsletter, a family newsletter, a staff member in charge of communications, and so forth. These arguments will often make sense in the competition for scarce dollars. But you shouldn't believe them. If your budget is cut drastically, the system may have to give up its own vehicles for disseminating its messages. Schools then become dependent upon the news media, parent organization newsletters, and the like. Of course, using the mass media is the fastest and cheapest way to reach the public, and in the midst of a crisis you'll no doubt be working with reporters and editors to do just that. But without your own budget and your own vehicles for sending your messages out, you have no way to get follow-up explanations and in-depth information out to school patrons and the larger community. You have very little chance to explain programs, ask for help with taxing initiatives, or appeal for understanding.

Protect your budget as best you can, and do not be misled by the penny-pinching arguments. Explore advertising, sponsorships, and grants in order to fund your program. Communication is important—it's the link between community support for education and the substantive work educators do in preparing students for their individual futures and for the collective future of all of us.

In the central office, more than in individual schools, monitoring the effectiveness of your program is key to demonstrating the value of your position, staff, and program. To prevent or minimize budget cuts, you must be prepared to provide evaluative data about your work. The next chapter provides many simple suggestions for doing so.

# 9

# Evaluating Your Communications Program

If everything you do counts, then count everything you do.

This chapter outlines a few basic, practical methods for collecting and presenting data about the effectiveness of your communications efforts. Often without special training, teachers who happen to be good writers or principals with a special talent for community relations may be pressed into service in communications. If you are one of these, you may not be familiar with accountability measures for communications. You may have been so busy *doing* the work that you have not thought much about *measuring* the effects of the work. But we live in the age of accountability, and evaluation of school programs has become a way of life.

So you must now be prepared not only to do your work but to defend it. In evaluating your program's effectiveness, you have several options. All are costly, not so much in dollars as in staff time and expertise. This chapter

concentrates on the simple and inexpensive options, but you'll also find information about the more complex and expensive options, which are often necessary.

## Reviewing Strategic Goals

First, at both school and system levels, review your communications goals and objectives, then look at the various strategies and tactics you are employing to achieve each one. If you have developed your own plan, the chances are that you have established a set of goals both comprehensive and continuous. You can simply take stock of the outcomes of your work—that is, make judgments about whether your efforts have fulfilled the goals and where you may need to put more effort. Then you can translate your judgments about effectiveness into a written report for your administrators, attaching any documentation you have.

Annually you will probably also be updating the strategies and tactics to reflect new challenges within the overall plan. (See the sample communications plans in Appendixes A and B.) Such updates can also be included in your report. In addition, the following suggestions about tallying audience impressions and the services provided may be useful in giving actual data about your efforts. Another possible addition is the inclusion of selected newspaper clippings or video clips tracking stories or issues over the year and showcasing your efforts.

## Listing Services Provided

To account for everything, begin by listing the continuous *services* required to achieve your strategic goals—not the strategies nor the results. Listing the services will help you see the differing aspects of your work clearly and will greatly expedite your ability to prepare reports.

Here, for your review, is a list of examples, although your program may offer other or different services. Systemwide programs often provide all the services listed; school-based services are typically concentrated in "News and Information Services," with the addition of preparing newsletters from "Editorial Services" and on-site photography from "Photographic Services." In addition, school-based staff often provide assistance with "Special Events" and with "Consultative Services" with their colleagues at the school. Just adapt this list to

describe the services you offer, and add others as applicable.

• *News and Information Services.* Writing news releases; making media calls; arranging news conferences; handling on-camera interviews; researching and responding to inquiries (including responses to requests for information from parents and citizens); making arrangements for on-camera work.

• *Editorial Services.* Preparing print, audiovisual, and multimedia materials: writing/editing newsletters and executive bulletins; writing and coordinating home page text, including graphic design and guidelines; preparing fact sheets and special bulletins for various crises or emergencies; writing/editing op-ed pieces, speeches, and scripts; writing superintendent's columns for community newsletters, letters to the editor, etc.; coordinating video production, including concept papers, scripts, etc.; scripting and directing multimedia presentations.

• *Executive Services.* Writing correspondence and speeches; preparing computer-assisted or multimedia presentations; planning special events; holding news conferences; writing/editing op-ed pieces; arranging meetings with editors and reporters; scripting videos and presentations; researching issues; preparing materials for presentations; handling legislative liaison work; handling executive gift selections.

• *Design Services.* Providing technical assistance in graphic design, including generating design and production specifications for print materials; preparing optional designs for print and electronic materials; producing camera-ready copy; overseeing the print process; consulting with school employees on design issues.

- *Photography Services.* Providing technical assistance in photography, including taking photographs, overseeing their development, maintaining stock photo files, selecting the best shots for use in publications, and consulting with school employees on aspects of photography.

- *Event Planning.* Planning and coordinating special events, such as new school dedications, awards banquets, recognition ceremonies, major meetings for the superintendent and school board, and important conferences, including arrangements, speakers, locations, programs, themes and decorations, door prizes, and so forth.

- *Displays and Exhibits.* Providing displays and exhibits to take school information to shopping malls, conferences, and meetings, and to commemorate special recognitions and celebrations, such as American Education Week and the like.

- *Consultative Services.* Developing training programs; conducting meetings with school staffs and administrative staffs on public relations issues, such as giving advice about the layout and wording of a brochure about a new program; providing expertise about communications topics to colleagues or community members, such as conversations with principals about the wording of a letter to be sent to parents after a crisis or emergency.

- *Review and Advisory Services.* Providing reviews of manuscripts and résumés; arranging and conducting focus group meetings, reader surveys, opinion polls, and any other assessment activities.

The next step is to devise an easy way to tally the numbers for reporting your efforts. That's the purpose of Figures 9.1 through 9.6 (at the end of this chapter, pp. 92–95), which more or less correspond to this list of services.

## Counting Everything You Do

If everything you do counts, then count everything you do. Numbers convey precision; they are easily compared; their presence in your reports shows that you not only know the score, you keep score. Evaluation *means* counting.

If you are working in central office, weekly or monthly reports in tabular form help you to collect data routinely as part of normal office procedures. Such records can serve as the basis of compilations of the data for annual reports to the superintendent and school board. You may also find the collected data useful in presentations to professional and community groups when you are explaining your efforts. The sample forms (Figures 9.1–9.6) illustrate easy ways to collect data; feel free to change them to meet the needs of your program. These forms will help you keep up with the numbers of publications printed and mailed out, the numbers of phone inquiries, the numbers in each audience, the numbers of times each service is performed, and so on. You may also consider establishing a database to keep track of this information.

If you are working in a school, the sample reports suggested for your use are Figures 9.1 and 9.2. As a rule, school accountability does not require the same number of forms or tallies as central office accountability. Further, if you are a media liaison, your program coordinator may have spelled out accountability measures: a minimum number of news releases per month, a log of activities such as media calls, and files of clippings, for example.

For the services you provide infrequently, a chart with cells large enough to write in will enable you to note your actions specifically and to tally numbers of times performed or number of hours spent without quite as much detail. In fact, you may not need special forms at all. Especially at the school level, an ordinary desk calendar with large cells for each day, reserved for this use, is just right for recording phone calls, releases distributed, and the like, if you can keep your tallies straight and uncluttered by other notes.

## Understanding Audience Impressions

Most of the forms will yield straightforward tallies, but the concept of "audience impressions" (see Figure 9.2) needs some explanation. In determining audience impressions for your newsletter for families, for example, tally the print order for each issue. That number is an audience impressions estimate. At the end of the year, total the print orders for all the issues, and you will have the number for the year. For video programs, be guided by the number claimed as audience by your cable community station or by your local network affiliates. For newspaper articles, editorials, and op-ed pieces, the estimate you claim is the circulation of the newspaper. Once you have the circulation numbers for each media outlet, you can total all of them into one large number—this is the total number of audience impressions for the year.

Audience impressions are not the *actual* numbers of people who received or read or viewed the message you sent out—they provide an *estimate* of the audience you addressed. You really have no way to give a specific count for how many newsletters were read, for you never know which copies wound up on the floor of the birdcage. You simply report the numbers of the audience you addressed, and you must be completely open and comfortable about how you have arrived at the estimates. Because these numbers are estimates, you will need to balance them with more specific numbers, in terms of people who attend forums, workshops, presentations, and the like. But even there, you will usually be estimating the number rather than taking a head count. You may be more comfortable giving a range, such as 25 to 50 or 200 to 250, because the range itself implies that the number is only an estimate, not a head count.

## Tracking Your Work

Clippings files are the most basic of all tracking techniques, enabling you to demonstrate just what kinds of coverage your school or system received, and at whose hands. It is important to decide, on the front end, just which newspapers and tabloids you will review daily or weekly—most likely all in your community. Be sure to include minority and ethnic group publications, military newspapers, and civic tabloids, all of which can yield valuable perspectives. If you have the resources, you should consider clipping from regional, state, and national newspapers also, because their news coverage is likely to provide a broader perspective than the hometown papers. The various levels of coverage are helpful in tracking issues and policy topics; these you can incorporate into your issues management approach, alerting the superintendent and school board to developments that may affect decision making in the days ahead.

Maintaining clippings files is costly in terms of your time, so set your criteria for clipping carefully. Within a school, you need to clip only stories about your school. For the system, however, you have much greater range. You may decide, for example, to clip stories and editorials about major issues—the pieces you will need for tracking issues in the community—and not sports events, proms, and spelling bees. Or you may decide to clip and file every item pertaining to the system and all the schools—if you have sufficient staff, of course.

At the central office, an important decision is how you will develop and maintain your overall file. You will need two kinds of files: (1) the actual clippings and photocopies, dated, accurately referenced as to source and page numbers, and arranged in folders according to topics; and (2) a database on the computer, so that you can locate the articles you will later want by topic, title, date, publication, and author. At the school level, your files usually consist of the actual clippings and their photocopies.

Online services are a valuable addition to clippings files; they enable you to access print media online. These services can be especially useful in accessing news and editorial coverage in regional, state, and national newspapers. In addition, the larger papers maintain Web sites that offer daily access to the news of the day. However, it is not usually effective to substitute online services for clippings files entirely. There will always be a need for the actual clipping later, when you prepare copies so the superintendent or school board can see how the treatment of the story progressed.

Just as clippings files are useful, so is a collection of video clips of news reports. Various commercial video services are available, for a fee, of course, to provide the clips you need. Also, as a cost-saver, you can arrange with staff persons to record newscasts and shows pertinent to your collection. Collecting video clips and filing them requires the same thought as establishing clippings files for print articles. Once the cartridges threaten to outrun shelf space, you will need a computer database for recording topic, names of on-air personalities, source, date, and any cross-references for future uses. It is actually best to begin the database early—before you run out of shelf space.

Of course, video and print files serve purposes other than accountability. Clippings from the hometown paper, accompanied by a letter of congratulations from the superintendent, serve as an excellent public relations technique. Video clips of prominent community leaders discussing school topics are terrific enclosures with thank-you letters from the superintendent.

Your ability to demonstrate the development of important stories over time and to show the stories your office pitched to the media or the editorials you influenced behind the scenes is invaluable when it's time to illustrate the functions of the office. These additions can be enclosed along with your monthly or annual reports—an effective way to showcase a few specific results of your work.

## Keeping Up with and Reporting Costs

As you administer the budget for your program, you should keep up with the actual price of every endeavor. Your purchase orders, print orders, and vendor contracts will provide the financial information. Dividing the larger figure by the number in the audience or in the print order enables you to derive a per-copy cost, the most commonly publicized figure in print media.

It is important to publicize the costs in a judicious and savvy way. It's a good idea to be straightforward and open about the costs of print publications in particular, because their costs seem to be a lightning rod for complaints from the school board, the superintendent, and the public. Armed with the actual costs per piece, you can say calmly, "It's worth 10 cents per person, isn't it, to get this message out?" or "We've looked at other ways of publicizing summer school, but this is the least expensive . . ." and then go into detail.

## Conducting Surveys

Reader surveys can be simple and easy, like a 10-item set of questions included with a newsletter, with no concern for sampling techniques, just the hope that some readers will let you know what they like and what they'd like to change about the publication. Or they can be major undertakings requiring the technical skills of statisticians and item-response experts. Surveys can be accomplished by mail and supplemented with phone interviews; many surveys are conducted entirely by phone. For phone interviews, you can prepare a structured set of questions and response sheets, so that responses can be tallied, and involve everyone on the staff in conducting the interviews.

If you have access to an office of research and evaluation, the staff members there can assist you in conducting scientifically respectable surveys based on standard sampling techniques. Such surveys will yield reasonably defensible data as to what your readers prefer. The survey experts can also determine the number of phone interviews you will need to complement the mail survey data. Their assistance is also critically important in constructing the questionnaire and interview protocol for such an effort. With so much technical assistance necessary, many central office staffers reserve large reader surveys for rare occasions; in fact, such large surveys, because they are expensive, may be restricted to public opinion polls, which usually provide feedback on emerging issues within the community.

If you have to choose between expending resources on either reader surveys or public opinion polls, for example, you will probably consider that you get more for your money with the public opinion polls, because they can assist the superintendent and school board in determining the community's response to large issues and topics of concern. If you do not have adequate technical expertise within the system, you have the option of outsourcing your public opinion polls. (See Appendix J for sources.)

## Convening Focus Groups to Evaluate Publications and Videos

Focus groups can provide specific yet systematic feedback about publications and videos. In Appendix E, you'll find guidelines on how to conduct focus groups for this purpose. Plan to collect two types of information—a group

survey and individual comments. The group survey, often collected in a Likert-style instrument (*strongly agree* _____, *agree* _____, *disagree* _____, *strongly disagree* _____), is important because it enables you to keep the data from year to year and to compare results over time. The individual comments are just as important because they enable you to see what is really on the minds of the readers and viewers. The comments can be compiled, classified, and then compared from year to year as well.

## Selecting Accountability Strategies

For many people, the entire slate of possible strategies may come across as impossible, even though the emphasis here has been on the doable and least costly. Do not attempt everything at once—there *is* far too much for a one- or two-person office or a school media liaison to contemplate. Just make every effort to choose *where* to begin. Start small and keep it simple: concentrate on numbers for various audiences, costs of all publications, basic clippings files, annual focus groups, and annual updates of your own strategic plan or the systemwide strategic plan. As these processes become automatic, you can extend and expand them to include the more ambitious counting schemes. The important thing in today's world is to have an accountability approach—don't leave home without one.

## Another View of Accountability

Another way to look at these accountability strategies is to view them as a way for you to see for yourself what you've accomplished (and add to your own performance portfolio). All those words and numbers that you gather in your tallies, surveys, focus groups, and reports are testimony to the effort you've put in and the work you've done on behalf of your school or system. If you've done a good job, you can remind yourself that the steps you've taken to establish and implement an effective communications program will have wide-reaching influence—assuring smooth operations, enhancing the image of public education, and building strong relationships both within the schools and between the schools and the families and communities they serve. Give yourself a pat on the back. You deserve it!

**Figure 9.1.**
**News and Information Services—Sample Weekly Report for Central Office or Schools**

Week of _____

| Services | Monday | Tuesday | Wednesday | Thursday | Friday | Total |
|---|---|---|---|---|---|---|
| News releases | | | | | | |
| Media calls | | | | | | |
| Research | | | | | | |
| On-camera interviews | | | | | | |
| Requests, with responses | | | | | | |
| Arrangements for media visits | | | | | | |
| News conferences | | | | | | |
| Other: _____ | | | | | | |

**Figure 9.2.**
**Audience Impressions—Sample Monthly Report for Central Office or Schools**

Month of _____

| Vehicles | Week 1 | Week 2 | Week 3 | Week 4 | Week 5 | Total |
|---|---|---|---|---|---|---|
| Newspaper stories | | | | | | |
| TV stories | | | | | | |
| Parent newsletter | | | | | | |
| Employee newsletter | | | | | | |
| Opinion leader bulletins | | | | | | |
| Special events | | | | | | |
| Community relations events | | | | | | |
| Parenting workshops | | | | | | |
| Other: _____ | | | | | | |

**Figure 9.3.**
**Editorial Services—Sample Weekly Report for Central Office**

Week of _____

| Services | Monday | Tuesday | Wednesday | Thursday | Friday | Total |
|---|---|---|---|---|---|---|
| Op-ed pieces, speeches, scripts | | | | | | |
| Columns, letters to editor | | | | | | |
| Newsletters, executive bulletins | | | | | | |
| Fact sheets | | | | | | |
| Video scripts, concept papers | | | | | | |
| Multimedia presentations | | | | | | |
| Home page preparation | | | | | | |
| Other: _____ | | | | | | |

### Figure 9.4.
### Executive Services—Sample Weekly Report for Central Office

Week of _____

| Services | Monday | Tuesday | Wednesday | Thursday | Friday | Total |
|---|---|---|---|---|---|---|
| Speech writing | | | | | | |
| Op-ed pieces | | | | | | |
| Meetings with media | | | | | | |
| Scripting videos and presentations | | | | | | |
| Research on issues | | | | | | |
| Preparation of materials for presentations | | | | | | |
| Legislative liaison activity | | | | | | |
| Executive gift selections | | | | | | |
| Other: _____ | | | | | | |

### Figure 9.5.
### Additional Services—Sample Weekly Report for Central Office

Week of _____

| Services | Monday | Tuesday | Wednesday | Thursday | Friday | Total |
|---|---|---|---|---|---|---|
| Design services | | | | | | |
| Photography services | | | | | | |
| Event planning | | | | | | |
| Displays and exhibits | | | | | | |
| Consultative services | | | | | | |
| Review and advisory services | | | | | | |
| Other: _____ | | | | | | |

**Figure 9.6.**
**Phone/Fax Log—Sample Weekly Report for Central Office**

Week of _____

| Services | Monday | Tuesday | Wednesday | Thursday | Friday | Total |
|---|---|---|---|---|---|---|
| Requests for information | | | | | | |
| Publications mailed out | | | | | | |
| Faxed information | | | | | | |
| Requests referred to appropriate office | | | | | | |
| Other: _____ | | | | | | |

# 10

# Think Courtship

You catch more
flies with honey
than with vinegar
—Old Saying

I hope you've found this book a storehouse of practical ideas for building support for schools, with ample encouragement for creating your own do-it-yourself communications program. Here's a last look at a few major concepts:

• *Learn to Take the Initiative.* Schools usually take care of communications during a crisis, but that's a *reaction.* Taking the initiative means being *proactive.* If you're proactive, you'll pay attention to *baseline* communications—the everyday efforts to stay in touch with all your constituents.

• *In Planning, Start Where You Are.* The planning process is important for two reasons.

First, planning helps you to become proactive, as you learn to anticipate information needs, analyze your varied audiences, and assess the vehicles for reaching them. Second, these elements of planning give you a big-picture framework to be sure you've covered all bases. Still, don't let the *tail* of planning wag the *dog* of communications. Keep the elements of planning in mind, use what you can, then add others as you have time.

• *Avoid Silence.* On the communications continuum, there's a no-talk end. Not talking to someone means a personal relationship is in limbo or in trouble—it's going nowhere or it's over. Failure to communicate means those involved aren't even trying to maintain a relationship. That's why silence is not the ticket for building support for schools. Silence tells people we don't care.

- **Think Courtship.** On the other end of the continuum, when you want to pursue or strengthen a relationship, you instantly become proactive, and very creative. Suppose, for example, you are attracted to a certain person. You'll communicate through phone calls, notes, e-mail, cards, flowers, private jokes, billboard ads, dinners out, dinners in, presents—even extrasensory perception. You'll present yourself in the best possible light. It's the courtship end of the continuum. To cultivate support, school leaders need to move toward this end.

- **Remember: Quality Comes Before Image.** Of course, no amount of great communication can make up for deficiencies in school climate or programs. Communications strategies, no matter how polished and professional, are no substitute for quality in school services, programs, staff, resources, and environment. The reality of the school must be just as good as, or even better than, the image of the school. Quality always comes first.

- **Integrity Is Your Best Bet.** In your efforts, always tell the truth. At the same time, avoid the educator's habit of explaining too much. Learn to be concise and to the point, without elaboration, when you answer questions. Always observe the boundaries of good taste and confidentiality. Your integrity is at stake, and leaders who demonstrate integrity

build confidence in schools far more effectively than those who rely on any false stance.

- **Communications Efforts Are Another Kind of Teaching.** In teaching, we impart different messages (content knowledge and skills from the curriculum) to different audiences (individual students, specific classes, and grade levels) through a variety of media. We listen to our students, too, so we can match what we're teaching with their backgrounds and interests. In communications, it's much the same. We send varied school messages to varied audiences in a variety of media. In turn, we listen to people to understand and act on issues and preferences important to them. This similarity makes it easy for us to organize communications programs of considerable sophistication and to develop confidence in our own abilities to reach out to our communities and teach our varied audiences about our schools.

- **Cumulative Effects Yield Long-Term Results.** The analogy with teaching also holds when we look at long-term results. In the classroom, one outstanding lesson, one terrific unit, and one breakthrough with a student are not enough. Effective teaching is a matter of cumulative effects, doing the right thing today, tomorrow, and every day, so that student knowledge grows and deepens over time. Effective communications are the same. It's the cumulative effects that yield long-term results in gaining and strengthening school support.

- **Every Day, Inch Toward Success.** Working for cumulative effects may make you feel like Sisyphus, who kept pushing that rock up the mountain, only to have it fall back down. But take heart. Every day is a new opportunity to build long-term support for education. Every day we can help our schools continue and build on their present successes in achieving their intellectual, social, emotional, civic, and economic missions. Every day is another chance to think courtship, to make friends before we need them, and to build support for our schools.

# A Sample School Communications Plan

## Goal I: Provide information about school programs, events, and activities.

*Audience:* Parents, caregivers, and families.

*Strategy 1:* Provide welcome packets for new families whenever new students enroll and to all families at the beginning of each school year: school calendar, emergency communications plan, bus schedule and routes, staff lists, etc.
*Vehicle:* Routine information packaged in school folders, with letter welcoming patrons.

*Strategy 2:* Send weekly newsletters with up-to-date meeting notices, class news and activities, menus, and parenting tips.
*Vehicle:* School newsletters.

*Strategy 3:* Provide program brochures about each faculty and staff member, explaining their programs and credentials.
*Vehicle:* One-page desktop-designed brochures.

*Strategy 4:* Improve conferencing techniques. Schedule conferences at convenient times to suit individual parent schedules. Include students in conferences as appropriate.
*Vehicle:* Training sessions/conference days.

*Strategy 5:* Expand into electronic communications. Determine feasibility of homework hot line and install, if possible; select software, develop procedures, and design and implement school home page.
*Vehicle:* In-school planning and budgeting processes.

## Goal II: Provide information about student progress, student learning, and achievement.

*Audience:* Parents, caregivers, and families.

*Strategy 1:* Prepare and send report cards and interim progress reports promptly.

*Strategy 2:* Provide faculty with pads of notepaper for notes to parents and families.

*Strategy 3:* Prepare school profile data: enrollment; grade-level breakdowns; number on free and reduced price lunch, in special education, in gifted and talented program; student achievement test scores for past five years; distribute in parent newsletters, bulletins to opinion leaders, and reports to superintendent.

*Strategy 4:* Train all new faculty in conferencing techniques.

## Goal III: Provide information about helping children learn about the world around them and succeed in school.

*Audience:* Parents, caregivers, and families.

*Strategy 1:* Include parenting tips in school newsletter and on home page, such as help with homework, recommended books for different ages, safety and health topics, and educational activities in the community and surrounding area.
*Vehicle:* Newsletter, home page, community meetings.

*Strategy 2:* Inform parents and families about state content and performance standards, relationship to our local curriculum and textbooks, and state assessment programs.
*Vehicle:* Standards Seminar Series: monthly except December.

*Strategy 3:* Invite parent participation in classroom activities, library activities, museum events and exhibits, field trips, and special events.
*Vehicle:* Invitations from faculty.

## Goal IV: Develop a sense of belonging for all students.

*Audience:* Students.

*Strategy 1:* Issue a membership packet to all students at the beginning of the school year or when they enroll in school, including a membership card, coupons from local businesses, pennant, pencils and pens, folder with school rules, invitations to join clubs and teams, alerts about upcoming athletic events, picnics, trips, yearbook committees, etc.
*Vehicle:* Packets.

*Strategy 2:* Give each student new to the school a mentor who is an "old-timer." Train mentors in providing support for the new student for one year from date of entry. Ensure that mentors and new students regularly have time for getting together.
*Vehicle:* Selecting/training students; matching with incoming students.

*Strategy 3:* Implement student recognition initiative through displays of student work in all commons areas, selection for special attention such as lunch with the principal, citizen of the week and month and year, photo scrapbooks of all students in each class, etc.
*Vehicle:* Teacher committee, grade-level chairs.

## Goal V: Maintain proactive efforts to secure positive media coverage and attention.

*Audience:* The community in general.

*Strategy 1:* Maintain and continuously update lists of media contacts.
*Vehicle:* Secretary.

*Strategy 2:* Train staff in writing news releases, update release form and school logo for new school year, and issue news releases at least weekly; compile binders of news releases and display in parent resource center and school office.
*Vehicle:* Releases and binder; training as needed.

**Strategy 3:** Send thank-you letters from students and principal to reporters and editors for every positive or fair story. Send copies of clippings with "From the desk of..." memos to community leaders and school board members.
**Vehicle:** Student letters, letters from principal.

## Goal VI: Foster a productive workplace and enhance employees' professionalism and sense of community.

**Audience:** School employees.

**Strategy 1:** Maintain an "open door" policy on the part of the principal and assistant principals.

**Strategy 2:** Provide business cards and brochures for all staff and faculty, describing their school programs, school responsibilities, and credentials.
**Vehicle:** Cards and brochures created with desktop publishing.

**Strategy 3:** Provide training for all faculty for their role as ambassadors of goodwill for the school.

**Vehicle:** In-school staff development.

**Strategy 4:** Provide updated announcements, recognitions, and staff development notices.
**Vehicle:** Weekly staff bulletin.

**Strategy 5:** Provide customer service training for all new employees.
**Vehicle:** Training sessions, as needed.

## Goal VII: Create a parent volunteer program in cooperation with the PTA.

**Audience:** Parents, caregivers, teachers, students.

**Strategy 1:** Assess needs of teachers and expertise of parent and grandparent volunteers; match needs with areas of expertise and make assignments.
**Vehicle:** Survey of parents, caregivers, grandparents, and teachers.

**Strategy 2:** Provide orientation and training for volunteers and teachers.
**Vehicle:** Training sessions.

# A Sample Systemwide Communications Plan

*Note:* These goals are ongoing, continuous goals, not the narrowly focused goals of some systemwide, overall or strategic plans. The type of plan illustrated here requires an annual update to deal with new challenges, set priorities for the year, and check off accomplishments.

## Goal I: Raise public and employee awareness of systemwide events, programs, services, and goals.

*Strategy 1:* Develop and maintain procedures for routine communication functions.

a. Create working calendar of events for interoffice use on paper and on line.

b. Establish a master production calendar to include all publications and TV shows.

c. Update lists of media contacts four times yearly; distribute.

d. Provide staff development sessions for all administrators and media liaisons; four sessions for administrators (one required, three voluntary) and two sessions for media liaisons (required). Update their information about policies, procedures, changes, etc.

*Strategy 2:* Update and distribute procedures

for emergency and crisis situations.

a. On list of media contacts, indicate those with specific emergency responsibilities.

b. Maintain/update list of procedures for specific emergency situations.

c. Maintain file of disaster drills for each school and for every other district facility.

d. Maintain contact with emergency management offices and city departments; keep an up-to-date list of locations of hazardous sites; maintain files of action plans for emergency management.

e. Develop sample school handbook for assistance with emergencies at schools; distribute to principals for review and feedback; budget funds for production and for staff development in next school year.

*Strategy 3:* Coordinate central office efforts with school-based information strategies.

a. Exchange information daily or as needed: superintendent's office, all principals, legislative liaison, staff in community relations, and staff in pupil personnel management. Improve reliability of incident reporting process.

b. Present delineation of school-based and central office functions to media liaisons during training sessions; seek feedback; improve understanding of who does what.

c. Provide staff development on school board policies related to media and community relations, orientation to the communications program, and an overview of the services and functions provided by the staff.

*Strategy 4:* Support the initiatives of the superintendent and the school board.

a. Assist with superintendent's routine and specialized correspondence; maintain computer files of sample letters; develop handbook and diskette of form letters.

b. Prepare superintendent's speeches; deliver in presentation binders with supporting information about the event: place, time, day, organization, name of contact on site, other honored guests and community leaders likely to attend.

c. Prepare op-ed pieces for the local paper to explain initiatives and support marketing campaigns.

d. Publicize board meetings, issues under consideration, and subsequent actions.

e. Organize specific marketing campaigns regarding use of technology in schools and capital and operating budget needs.

*Strategy 5:* Identify newsworthy events and programs, and prepare media campaigns to support or publicize them.

a. Coordinate editorial needs of media contacts with school system efforts.

b. Collaborate with colleagues to showcase accomplishments.

## Goal II: Build information-sharing capacity within schools and the community.

*Strategy 1:* Maintain print, electronic, and video vehicles for internal and external audiences.

a. Update specifications for all print materials: parent and family newsletter, employee newsletter, bulletin for opinion leaders, annual report, and brochures. Seek bids for print services, evaluate, and make selection.

b. Update design and content of annual report and brochures—solicit changes from administrators, update copy, and seek approval of edited copy from the responsible administrators.

*Strategy 2:* Develop systemwide master calendar of events.

a. Initiate design and production of master calendar on paper and on computer.

b. Contact community groups for input into master calendar; collect data.

c. Determine best place in organization for continuous calendar updating.

*Strategy 3:* Increase staff participation in professional writing and presentations.

a. Develop staff resource list matching personnel with their special organizations.

b. Collect news of staff talents, exemplary teaching and administration efforts, local responses to issues and trends in education, and the like, in order to recommend school employees for specific writing and presentation opportunities.

**Strategy 4:** Provide staff development to support information-sharing and public information functions.

a. Provide consultative services to meet school and system needs.

b. Design or contract for staff development sessions as needed.

**Strategy 5:** Network with parent association members, parents not in organized groups, community leaders, business and industry representatives, military representatives, professional association representatives, and reporters and editors to exchange information and concerns.

a. Recommend school employees for membership and leadership in such groups.

b. Organize issues management approach based on shared information; forward concerns to superintendent.

c. Offer extra copies of school publications for distribution at meetings.

d. Publicize news of promotions of school employees, departmental changes, and new functions and goals of the school system.

## Goal III: Increase public awareness of issues, trends, and resources in education.

**Strategy 1:** Develop and maintain a speakers' bureau for community events and programs.

a. Maintain lists of school employees and their areas of expertise.

b. Publicize the list and the topics to community organizations.

c. Encourage the creation of interactive and multimedia presentations to community groups, in order to model learning strategies used in schools and encourage participation.

d. Publicize procedures for use of school facilities to community groups, and encourage meetings in facilities to showcase or explain curriculum, instruction, and student achievement.

**Strategy 2:** Encourage the participation of educators on community boards, in community organizations, and in professional associations.

a. Recommend educators to fill vacancies on community boards, etc.

b. Publicize availability of positions within community organizations.

c. Coordinate with issues management process, and forward shared information about concerns to superintendent.

**Strategy 3:** Provide targeted presentations and public information campaigns, as needed, on such topics as parenting, discipline, budget development and administration, etc.

a. Determine needs within the system, and identify sources of expertise.

b. Design and produce the campaigns.

**Strategy 4:** Increase the leadership role of the schools in the community and the state.

a. Increase the visibility and leadership of school employees.

b. Provide technical assistance to sharpen the performance of school employees in presentations and publications.

c. Provide packets of print materials for distribution at professional meetings.

*Strategy 5:* Develop and maintain issues management processes.

    a. Conduct focus groups on emerging issues; identify concerns.

    b. Maintain position papers and quotations from appropriate administrators on pertinent topics.

    c. Share information from community with superintendent.

    d. Add legislators to distribution lists for news releases and print materials.

*Strategy 6:* Support the school or system image and identity in the design and presentation of publications, documents, and displays.

    a. Develop and maintain audience profiles representing both external and internal audiences and including the varied community constituencies.

    b. Recognize and showcase the accomplishments of school employees.

    c. Develop an inventory of publications, including provisions for storage, distribution, retrieval, and displays; develop lists of contents of packets for various audiences.

    d. Draw on information in master calendar to schedule presentations and displays for community events.

## Goal IV: Monitor the effectiveness of the plan.

*Strategy 1:* Maintain clippings file and computer database.

    a. Review topics for filing and procedures for clipping, and reassign tasks as necessary.

    b. Expand papers to be reviewed to include *The Washington Post.*

*Strategy 2:* Conduct focus-group and advisory panel sessions with representatives from target audiences to collect feedback about specific events, publications, and strategies.

    a. Prepare Likert-style questionnaires for focus groups to evaluate publications.

    b. Solicit diverse participants for focus group invitations: recommendations from principals, PTA president, and business partners.

    c. Prepare report on focus group feedback for superintendent's review.

*Strategy 3:* Prepare quarterly reports for the superintendent and school board.

    a. Maintain charts to show services provided and audience impressions. Keep monthly tallies of services provided and of audience impressions.

    b. Prepare packets to show tracking of major stories and issues to accompany numerical data. Include pertinent news releases.

# How to Write a News Release

In the media world, news releases are the work-horses of the profession. A well-crafted news release (or press release) is an excellent vehicle for conveying information to reporters and editors, and to school employees and community groups at the same time. This how-to discussion offers practical tips on writing news releases in case you are not a journalist by trade.

News releases may take several forms, including the following:

• "Regular" news releases—the topic of this appendix.

• Media alerts—very brief announcements of upcoming events, giving date, time, and place, with a few additional words to generate interest in coverage.

• Photo-op alerts—same as media alerts but emphasizing great pictures.

• Fact sheets—detailed information about a particular issue or topic; for example, a list of steps taken to clean a classroom after asbestos contamination. Can be independent of or attached to a regular news release.

• Internal bulletins—timely updates on a major issue such as how the system is coping with a major school fire or notices about professional opportunities.

Here are pointers for the preparation of news releases in general:

• Develop your own format for news releases, including the alternative forms. Keep your school or system logo consistent, but consider varying clip art to emphasize story content.

• Be sure your form includes all necessary information: school or system name and address, the date of release, phone number(s), fax number, and the name of the person(s) to call for more information. Reporters must be able to reach you quickly, but school phone lines are very busy and available only during limited hours. Because reporters are always in a time crunch, also give private line, home, and cell phone numbers. Cell phone numbers are especially important if your school group is going to a location without a phone—such as a riverbank for an on-location science lesson or a museum for a hands-on art activity. If reporters and editors can't reach you on location, and quickly, your event won't even be considered for coverage.

• Give the release a one- or two-line title. For routine releases, a simple descriptive headline will do, calling attention to what is newsworthy. Occasionally you can use two lines. Using a secondary line can give more information and therefore can be very effective.

• Keep it short. A release is not the place to tell all; a release is designed to get media coverage. Use a "For more information" line at the bottom to give access to someone who can provide the facts beyond the news release: "For more information, call Kerry Smith at xxx-xxxx."

• Always include the facts: the *who, what, where, when, why,* and *how.* Always give the day and date the event or news will happen (or happened), and give the precise time of day or the span of time. Remember, timing is everything for reporters and editors.

• Make your lead sentence catchy, if appropriate, or put some exciting ideas in at appropriate places. This may be the place for your "news hook," an entertaining or "hot" topic, the slant or spin by which you generate interest and get coverage. Avoid jargon; use plain English.

• Use short paragraphs, usually two or three sentences each. Long blocks of text are a turn-off. Reporters and editors are in a hurry, and the release should *look* and *be* easy to read.

• Use quotations from appropriate persons to convey part of the important information, not merely approval or recognition, if you can. Feel free to compose the quotations, but be sure each authority reviews and corrects any quotation attributed to him or her. Do not use any quotation not approved by the person it is attributed to. Remember the "no surprises" rule.

• Consider your purpose—do you want television cameras to cover an event? If so, include visual appeal—a huge facsimile of a check to represent a donation or a grant, a banner for the bazaar, children in costume. For TV, *think visually.* Get the release out well in advance of the event, so the assignment editors can schedule a camera crew. Then follow it with enthusiastic phone calls to assignment editors or reporters, to pitch the event. You can follow up with last-minute notices as well—quick alerts faxed the day of the event.

• On the other hand, if you want the newspaper to print a slate of officers for a club, you can send out the release after the officers were elected or installed.

• Remember the "For more information" line.

• End the release by centering "-30-" or "###" at the bottom of the page.

## Sample News Release #1: Soft, Good News

**Danville Teacher Named State Foreign Language Teacher of the Year**
*1997 Award Goes to Jane Doe of Danville High School*

On Saturday, November 8, in Capital City, Jane Doe will receive the title of "Foreign Language Teacher of the Year" for the State of Confusion. The occasion for the presentation of the award is the annual meeting of the Foreign Language Association of the State of Confusion, which selected Doe for the honor.

Doe, a 15-year veteran, now teaches French and Spanish at Danville High School, where in 1993 she was selected Danville Teacher of the Year and served as chair and member of several foreign language curriculum and textbook adoption committees.

In addition to her work at the school, Doe has sponsored student trips to France, Spain, and Mexico during five summers. In 1990 she was a participant in an institute sponsored by the National Endowment for the Humanities, "History and Literature of France," held in Washington, D.C. In 1991 she served on the Visiting Committee for the Upscale High School Ten-Year Self-Study in Upscale, Maine. She has attended numerous conferences sponsored by the Foreign Language Association and has often served as a workshop presenter at the conferences. Further, she consults with teachers of English as a Second Language for both adults and children. She is well known for her volunteer assistance to those who are newcomers to the United States, facilitating their efforts to overcome language misunderstandings and understand the various cultural influences they encounter in American life.

"We are pleased that Ms. Doe has received this recognition from the Foreign Language Association," said Melissa Exemplary, Superintendent. "She has an outstanding record of professional achievement and personal service. She has the respect of her peers, the affection of her students, and the appreciation of their parents for all she contributes to the education of their children."

For more information, call Howard T. Topguy, Principal of Danville High School, at (xxx) xxx-xxxx.

###

## Sample News Release #2: Hard, Fast-breaking News

### Damage Estimates Reach $3 Million in Central High School Fire

Estimates of the damages incurred in the March 24 fire at Central High School approach $3 million, according to figures just received by the Centralia School District from Paragon Insurance Company. The insurance adjuster for Paragon, Billy Ray Yodel, has worked closely with John Doe, Superintendent; Al Hardy, Director of School Facilities; and Mary Beancounter, Principal, since the morning of the fire.

"It's been a long and technical process to arrive at these estimates," said Hardy, "and there may be some changes in the numbers as the actual work progresses."

The $3 million estimate was calculated after architects and engineers made repeated inspections of the facility. They developed detailed assessments of what may be salvaged, as well as the costs of the preparations of all areas of the school for reoccupancy by students and teachers. The $3 million figure represents an estimate of the total insurance claim, including design fees, asbestos abatement, expenses for demolition and reconstruction, building contents, and other consequential damage.

Better Air, Inc. has prepared an asbestos abatement plan, which has been reviewed by Hardy and his staff. This plan will take about 90 days to execute and is estimated to cost $450,000. The asbestos abatement effort, scheduled to begin next week, is financed by Paragon Insurance Company and is included in the $3 million estimate.

In addition, Better Air, Inc. is completing plans for the restoration of the damaged areas. Preliminary projections call for this work to cost about $1,500,000, which is included in the $3 million total.

No firm date has been set for reoccupancy of the damaged portions of the building. The overall project schedule is directed toward reoccupancy when school opens in September. "It's impossible to predict a specific date for reoccupancy at this time," said Hardy, "but the reconstruction effort will continue to receive our full attention."

School principal Beancounter observes, "The teachers and students have made this unexpected transition into temporary quarters with amazingly good attitudes, and classes are taking place every day in all subjects. Our parent volunteers are continuing their excellent work, other schools have loaned copies of textbooks and materials, and the bag lunches are a big hit. We gratefully appreciate the outpouring of support from the community during this crisis."

For more information, call Hardy at (xxx) xxx-xxxx or Beancounter at (xxx) xxx-xxxx.

###

### Sample News Release #3: Internal Bulletin

**"Sex, Teens, and Public Schools" on WYTV-TV Examines Role of Public Education in Preventing Teen Pregnancy**

On Monday evening, October 23, at 10:00 p.m., WYTV-TV (Channel xx) will broadcast a one-hour program, hosted by Willa Celebrity, that deals with the role of public education in preventing teen pregnancy. The program, "Sex, Teens, and Public Schools," examines the issue of adolescent childbearing and the debate over the role of public schools in preventing early and unwanted pregnancy. The documentary features talks with parents, students, teachers, and health care providers and goes inside schools and prevention programs across the country. It presents both abstinence-only programs and those that offer a range of possible choices for teenagers.

If you have questions, please contact Pedro Goodsport, station manager, at (xxx) xxx-xxxx. A regular viewer line is available so that viewers can call at any time with their comments; the number is (xxx) xxx-xxxx.

### ###

# How to Develop Responsive Publications

So you want to start a newsletter, or a series of brochures for your school, or a student hand-book. Great! Just remember that your publica-tion will represent your school. If the newsletter is poorly designed, unattractive, and full of mis-spelled words, or if a brochure carries items that are out of date or incorrect, your school image will suffer. These hints will help you start off—and keep going—on the right foot.

## Clarifying Purpose and Audience

• Determine the purpose of, and the audi-ence for, the proposed publication. Think of the messages you want to send, then put your-self in the place of someone who will receive the publication and analyze what your informa-tion needs are as a member of the targeted audience. Look for overlaps between your mes-sages and the information needs of your audi-ence(s)—that's the best place to start writing. If there are no overlaps, strike a balance or divide the copy between what you need to say and what the audience wants to know.

• Determine the size or length of the publi-cation, the budget, the method of duplication (printing or photocopying), the number of copies needed, the number of issues per year and the schedule for each issue (including copy deadlines), the method of distribution to the audience(s), and distribution lists and procedures.

## Designing for Reader Appeal

• Identify your designer or desktop pub-lisher and develop sample layouts and logos (such as school symbols or mascots). If you will do your own design work, collect sample publi-cations and learn to analyze designs for appeal-ing elements and easy-to-read layouts. The following suggestions are basic.

• Learn to allow ample "white space." White space is inviting to the reader. Do not crowd the pages.

• Keep the *fonts* (styles of type) readable and simple. Most school audiences like fonts that resemble textbook styles. Do not use the fancy ones. Do not use tiny type. Do not use a variety of fonts. You want the publication to be easy to read.

• Consider *ragged right* margins (left-justified only) to create reader appeal, ease of reading, and informality.

• In general, use a predictable layout so readers know what to expect and can follow the text easily. Place regular features in the same locations in each issue, and use a familiar logo or simple clip art as an aid to identifying recurring items or columns. Take care not to let the artwork overpower the copy; rather, the artwork should enhance the copy.

• If you work with a printer, develop print specifications for your publications: size and type of paper, color of paper, number and identification of colors of ink, camera-ready copy, use of disks, etc. Work with a printer or copy house on the details and on costs. Get all your technical questions answered.

## Writing the News

• Analyze your audience for level of education, income level, recreational interests, favorite films and TV programs, ethnic diversity, and the like. Locate statistical information about your community: ask for statistical reports from the chamber of commerce, or review the local newspaper's reader profiles. Learn to sense audience preferences and information needs.

• In writing, strive for clear, conversational, jargon-free language suitable for your audience. Select a style manual, or develop one, for settling usage questions and developing consistency. Develop proofreading skills and procedures to support the steps in your production process. If you personally are not good at proofreading, find someone who is. Do not send out publications with grammatical or spelling errors in them.

• "Design" the copy so it's easy for the reader to follow: use bullets, short paragraphs, subheads, and white space. You can't tell everything you know about the topic; so always include a line like this: "For more information about the egg hunt, call the Easter Bunny at xxx-xxxx."

• Identify writers/stakeholders, editor, advisory group or editorial board, methods of news collection, sign-offs needed for approval before publication. Work with all stakeholders to understand the steps in the production process: e.g., Write, Edit, Review, Correct, Design, Proof, Correct, Prepare for Duplication.

• Learn to work with your writers/stakeholders (those who will be contributing copy). Ensure that edited copy is returned to your writers/stakeholders for their corrections and approval *before* the newsletter goes to the designer. The goal is to keep corrections to one round during the design process. In design, you and the designer will have to fit the copy to the space available, and you will find it necessary to make a few editing changes to do so. But if you are making extensive corrections during design, find out why and then insist on complete corrections in advance of design. Limiting the number of rounds of corrections will save time for an in-house designer, and dollars if you are outsourcing design services.

## Getting the Publication to Readers

Develop your distribution procedures, and reach agreement with the printer or copy house about schedules, turnaround time, delivery, bundling, and so forth. Communicate often with the printer, especially if you're behind schedule. Schedules are serious business for commercial printers. Keep the mail house informed, if you use one.

## After Your First Few Issues

Develop your editorial calendar a year in advance, if you can. Predict news stories for each issue, but be prepared to change as priorities shift. Make the copy deadlines known to all contributors. Avoid giving front-page coverage to statements from top administrators; put their messages on inside pages. Reserve the front page for news of prime interest to the reader.

When members of the audience for your newsletter begin to tell you about something they read in the publication, you'll know you've created a responsive publication. Enjoy!

# How to Conduct Focus Groups to Evaluate Publications

Eventually you'll want to evaluate your publications to see whether they're meeting the information needs of their varied audiences. Feedback from focus groups can improve your publications. These guidelines will make it easy for you to conduct a focus group to critique your work. Here are the basics:

• *Definition*—A focus group is a group of people who represent the audience for a specific publication (print or video), convened to give a friendly critique.

• *Purpose*—The purpose of convening a focus group is to get specific feedback about how well a publication (print or video) meets the information needs of its intended audience and, consequently, how to improve the publication.

• *Format*—The format is informal and social; the participants sit around a table or configuration of tables. Discussion is guided by a list of questions or an agenda, which serves to keep the group on task; but meaningful digressions are welcome. You may also find it necessary to provide copies of the newsletter or show the video, to gain specific responses to various features or stories.

## Inviting Members

• Start by developing a list of prospective members. You'll need members from all ethnic groups, income levels, regions, staff levels, and special interests. Ask colleagues for personal recommendations for members. Seek some members who do not normally have a highly visible presence rather than those who serve on every committee.

• Make personal phone calls to prospective members, based on personal recommendations from colleagues, and refer to the name of the person who made the recommendation. Confirm the prospect's correct phone number and mailing address. Indicate the possible date and place of the meeting. Then follow up with letters of invitation, giving all details including parking. Attach copies of anything you want reviewed in depth. These should arrive a week before the meeting.

## Conducting the Meeting

• Prepare your list of questions—only what you really need to know—or your agenda for the meeting. Prepare packets of copies of the publication, or arrange for viewing videotapes.

114

Prepare displays to show any recent or proposed changes in format, design, or layout, if necessary.

• Prepare simple questionnaires for collecting specific feedback, with a rating scale for features of this publication. (You want to be able to compare ratings over time.) Try out your questionnaires and rating scales with colleagues before the meeting to be sure you're asking the right questions, and clearly.

• As members of the focus group arrive, greet them, provide name tags, and offer simple refreshments. Thank everyone for coming, and start the meeting on time.

• Explain that the list of questions or the agenda is a guide; then begin the conversation about the questions or agenda items. Use a flip chart to record ideas, and keep the group on target by getting back to the list or agenda. Be comfortable with animated conversation and exchanges of opinion. Accept all suggestions without promising that all will be implemented. Remember you want honest feedback and honest differences of opinion.

• Take notes about the comments or, with everyone's permission, tape-record the discussion. End the meeting on time. Thank everyone for coming, and tell them what to expect next, in terms of mailing or duties, etc.

## After the Meeting

Within a week, follow up with thank-you letters, and attach reports showing how the ratings came out, along with a compilation of the comments. If your next newsletter or program shows how you used the group's feedback, send copies to the group members and demonstrate to them how important their comments were. Thank them again for their assistance.

## Reconvening the Focus Group

• It's not necessary, but you may want to retain the same members from year to year, adding new ones to ensure appropriate representation of the audience, as needed. Occasionally you will find that members feel honored by their selection and would like to remain in the group. Retaining some members yields a certain amount of continuity. Then, too, the group can become advocates of your publication, offering support for your school or program.

• Throughout the year encourage ongoing feedback from your audience. Try simple reader surveys, and always provide phone numbers for your office. Respond to all questions, complaints, and comments in friendly fashion; and consider each one a suggestion for improvement.

• Plan to convene a focus group at least once a year. You'll find participants' comments are your best source of feedback and promising avenues of improvement. If you want to know what works, ask the customer!

*Note:* There are other purposes for convening focus groups, such as identifying issues and concerns in the community. See Appendix J for resources.

# How to Produce a School Information Video

You've seen the videos developed for promotional purposes by the technology companies or the ones distributed by colleges or schools in your area. You're impressed with the amount of information and the positive image these videos provide for parents, prospective students, teachers—anyone. And now you'd like a school information video for your school.

A video presentation of the school can introduce parents and students, perhaps civic clubs and local organizations, to important information about the academic focus of the school; expectations for student conduct; discipline codes; before- and after-school activities, including child care; and invitations to join parent groups or become school volunteers. How to begin?

## Getting Started

• Develop a preliminary concept for your school video. Jot down notes to begin an outline of the major subdivisions of the video, such as academics, discipline, guidance, extracurricular activities, volunteer opportunities, and the like. Determine the audience: Parents? Students? Entire community? Clarify the major

purpose of the videotape: An overview of the school? General information? Recruiting students? Then set the target length—10 or 12 minutes, give or take a few. Writing down your preliminary plans is an excellent way to get started. The written concepts will give you something to share with your faculty and staff and will give them concrete objectives to respond to.

• Identify a model video you want to imitate in some way, and critique it. Figure out what's effective about the one you like, and then imagine how to improve it. Show this to your faculty and staff, or make it available for checkout over a period of several weeks. Ask for evaluative comments, so that you can see what they like, and so that they can think critically about the kind of video they want for their school.

## Finding the Technical Expertise and the Funds

• Unless you're a video editor or camera person by trade, your next task is to find the people with the necessary technical skills. You'll need to identify the video camera crew, the scriptwriters, the editing suite, the technical editor, and so on. Become familiar with the technical requirements. Make arrangements for all the technical services you will need, and project a preliminary schedule for the production, based on the best information you can get from your technical advisers.

• If you need funds from outside the school budget, it's best to identify a school partner who can assist with financing the production or to earmark a certain source, such as revenues from the sales of school supplies for a period of time, to be set aside for the production of the video. You need to consider the original costs of production, as well as the costs of duplication and distribution. Will the video be sent to real estate agents? If so, how many copies will that require?

• Determine who will be responsible for what—that is, who provides the "deliverables" to the school, who pays for copies, how many copies, and so forth. Secure the necessary approvals for your funding plan.

• If you find that your resources do not permit a professional production, perhaps you can identify a parent or an employee with very good skills with a camcorder. Such videos can be very effective, even though they are not broadcast quality.

## Getting Input from Faculty and Staff

• Conduct a meeting with your faculty and staff to get their input. Share your preliminary outline or list of topics and seek suggestions about those topics. In the beginning, be sure to caution everyone that the video will not be long enough to show everything that happens in the school. It will be necessary to omit some topics and some good ideas just to keep the video short enough to appeal to its audience. Ask what questions they hear from parents, students, and community members, and how they provide the answers. Ask what aspects of the school program they would like to see included in the video, but be consistent in emphasizing that the video will not be long enough to include everything.

## Completing the Plans

• Begin the development of your "storyboard," which is the overall plan for the production of the video itself. You'll need to plan the visuals alongside the script, of course. Devise a way to "save" good ideas, or use them in another way, but adhere to the target length.

• Develop the major subdivisions of topics and the concept of "scenes" within those major subdivisions. Begin to draft the script. Write the script in two columns, inserting the visual images you desire, such as "students working in chemistry lab," and identifying the scenes, such as "Mrs. Hubbard's third-period chemistry class, wearing goggles, surrounded by equipment; show Mrs. H. giving directions, students responding, then students at work in teams, replicating the exercise." Place the visuals in the left column and the full script in the right column. Have this stage of the script reviewed by appropriate faculty and staff, then revise accordingly. You'll find that paying attention to the script and the early identification of scenes will make the film better in the long run. You'll know exactly what footage is needed when you schedule camera crews to begin the process of filming in the school.

• Identify raw footage needs. What scenes do you need? Do you have any footage on hand? What quality is the footage? Once you are clear about the footage you need, make a list of it, correlated to the double-column script described above.

• Identify the narrator, who will be responsible for the voice-over narration of the script. This step requires you to listen carefully to a number of potential narrators. It is best to have people try out on the actual script, or the current draft. Other voices may be used in quotations or as natural parts of the scenes. For example, classroom scenes should draw from the teacher's lecture or instruction and from the students' responses. For the voice-over narration, however, you must consider carefully the professional quality of the voice, the delivery, and the tone. Consider the matter of gender very carefully. If you can balance female and male voices, your video will have greater appeal. Consider also whether the narration should sound very authoritative, very persuasive, or very matter of fact; at different points in the script, different tones may be appropriate. You may be able to secure the services of a professional broadcaster, especially if one of your school partners is a TV or radio station or if a station is willing to provide the service pro bono. You may also find a drama teacher who, even if he or she doesn't have the talent for

narration, may be able to identify people in the community who would be willing to try out.

• Design the title, credits, and scene dividers; determine the graphics to be used overall and for the transitions between scenes or major subdivisions. Collect or create the text for the title, scene dividers, and credits—any written material that will be needed—on a diskette.

## Schedule the Shoots, the Editing, and the Duplication

• Schedule the shoots and plan to get the scenes you need. You'll need to make arrangements with the teachers and the principal well in advance of each shooting. Allow several weeks for all the shooting. In fact, if you have a year, the extended time will enable you to get footage all year and then to incorporate scenes with different weather, different stages of instruction, and different seasonal events.

• Confirm the editing schedule with your technical support people. In the editing suite, you should work with the editor, side by side, to get the effects you want. You can have rough-cuts (the first drafts of video) reviewed by the faculty and staff, if necessary. However, if you do, you will probably need to schedule time for re-editing according to their suggestions.

## Celebrate Opening Night

Deliver the finished product to the faculty and staff. Arrange the first showing as a celebration of your school; make the occasion festive and appreciative. Thank everyone who participated in any way—it was a team effort, after all, and the important thing is that the school is well represented. Once copies are made, distribute them to the school board, superintendent, real estate agents, chamber of commerce, mayor's office, and other places where there's an audience for information about your school.

## Appendix G

# How to Create a Home Page

So you want your own Web site? Right on! With increased use of the Internet, school information just naturally belongs online. You'll be surprised at the hits you'll get—local parents seeking basic information about one school or trying to compare schools within the system; high school alumni trying to find out about reunions or tell former teachers about their successes; prospective employees looking for jobs; and families across the country assessing schools before they make the move to your town.

From the start, it's helpful to separate the instructional uses of the Internet from the communications and marketing purposes. The instructional uses, still in a fledgling state in most schools, are making possible new avenues for independent research, online interviews with experts, collaborative projects with classes next door or around the world, peer-reviewed exhibitions of student work, and worldwide exchanges of correspondence among teachers and students. These instructional purposes—along with developing technological literacy as an employment skill—constitute the

major reasons for the expansion of Internet access in schools, although the public information uses inevitably come forward.

### Policy Implications

Because the process is in its infancy, creating a home page carries with it a few unusual considerations, such as determining what information will go on the page and finding the technical expertise you need to get your page up and running. Consequently, you must plan for the policy implications. You will need to review existing board policies about electronic communications, privacy issues, access issues, and the like. In addition, consider parental involvement; for example, you will probably want a parental permission slip for the use of student names or likenesses on the Web site. Where you encounter gaps and deficiencies in existing policies, you will need to alert the superintendent and other administrators and begin the process of informing the school board and presenting new or amended policies and regulations to them for action.

## Accuracy and Authenticity

A home page is a publication and, as such, is subject to the same considerations as a newsletter or brochure; that is, the content must be accurate, the graphics must be appropriate, and the language use must be correct and sensitive. Misspelled words, an ungrammatical structure, or any phrase that can be interpreted negatively by any group will be just as damaging to the image of the school or school system as if they appeared in print publications.

It's important on the front end, also, to realize that official home pages will require administrative review, just as the school newsletter does, to ensure administrative approval. A home page will require regular updates, because nothing will be more annoying to those who visit your Web site than outdated information.

As for design questions, you will want to maintain consistency and continuity with print publications in the use of logos, fonts, and artwork. This will keep the school or system's visual images identifiable and assist viewers in recognizing that the home page belongs to your school or system, as well as letting them know that yours is the only official, authorized home page.

## Technical Matters

With these background issues settled, it's time to turn to the issue that can be a deterrent for communications specialists: the technical skills necessary for creating the home page.

What are the technical specifications you will follow? What hardware and software does the process of Web design require? Who is going to code the text, design the graphics, determine the menu choices, and establish the links with other sites? What software programs are most effective?

If you can answer these questions and do these tasks, you're in a great position. Otherwise, if you're lucky, you'll be able to recruit a school system employee, a volunteer parent, or a group of students skilled at both coding and design. There are software programs created especially for the design of Web sites; you may be able to find a computer-savvy volunteer who is, or can become, proficient in the use of such programs. Without such skill in the family, so to speak, your last resort may be to outsource the development, design, and periodic updating of your home page; that arrangement will depend on your spending money, of course, or on recruiting sponsors, if board policies permit advertising arrangements. For additional assistance, become a Web browser, and visit other sites to develop your own sense of effective design.

To simplify administrative review, it's a good idea to use text you have already generated and put through the approval process, such as the text from current publications. Using prepared text also has the advantage of consistency in the messages presented to the public through all media. You can use any number of current and customary publications as menu selections on your home page, such as parent newsletters, employee newsletters, school board member profiles, news releases, and program brochures. After all, electronic communication gives you a different vehicle for distribution, but the messages you have to send don't change because they're transmitted electronically. It's a good idea also to cross-reference your print publications on the Web so that viewers learn they can also receive the information in print by calling to request it.

For Web sites, your usual audience analysis will help you to shape the menu selections to address the information needs of the various audience segments. You will not need to name audience segments on the menu, because people will simply self-select what they want to know. Those who want to view profiles of school board members, for example, will go to that selection. On the other hand, those who want to check bus schedules or lunch menus will click on that selection. You may need to double-check your menu selections, just to be sure the home page does contain something for everyone who may be browsing the Web.

It is necessary to name your Webmaster on your home page, so that viewers of the home page can contact that person with any comments or questions. Present the Webmaster's e-mail address clearly, probably in the beginning and at the end. If you have a menu selection specifically for public comment about a timely topic, be sure the response boxes include the correct e-mail address and any pertinent time lines or expectations for the survey results to be reported online.

Be prepared to address additional editorial issues from time to time. For example, you may receive requests to insert personal and professional information, such as classified ads, association meetings, and items about births, deaths, degrees conferred, and the like. Set up the procedures for handling these requests just as you would for print publications, being guided by the procedures already in place for print materials.

You may also receive many requests for putting student work on the Web. Think through this issue with great care, especially the matter of audiences and the purpose of the home page. Student work, used as examples to show the results of instructional programs, can be especially valuable in conveying complete impressions about what goes on in classrooms. But when there's too much student work in an information source intended for the public, the work loses its appeal rapidly. You can facilitate the use of Intranets within each school or specific Web sites for teacher and student use, and you can create links to those sites for home page visitors who want an in-depth look at any particular student exhibition. For example, a page featuring the local science fair would further both instructional and public information purposes.

Schedule plenty of time for trial runs to ensure perfect operation before public announcements, and give your technical consultants all the support and assistance they need. Announce the launch of your home page at a school board meeting or major staff meeting, complete with news release and personal invitations to parent organization and teachers association officers, local policymakers, editors, and reporters. Be sure to arrange demonstrations of the Web site during this meeting; it's worth the trouble to give board members, administrators, teachers, and the public a close look at your home page and to show them how the menu selections work. Then don't forget: Publicize the URL in all your print publications, on stationery, and on television news.

*Note*: See Appendix J, "Resources," for information about the Family Education Network (FEN), which offers schools free assistance in developing Web sites.

## Appendix H

# How to Conduct Effective Parent-Teacher (-Student) Conferences

A parent-teacher (-student) conference is one of the most important relationship-building events in the school year, offering the great benefits of face-to-face communication. Conferences give parents or caregivers and teachers the chance to talk over the student's achievement, interests, study habits, attitudes toward different subjects, potential for improvement, and many other topics. Conferences are the main occasion for exchanging specific information and perspectives about an individual student's learning and achievement. It's a time when home and school get to know each other better. Yet conferences often cause consternation on the part of parents or caregivers, teachers, and students alike. Everyone has a reason to feel defensive or apprehensive, especially when conduct or learning or study habits are not what they should be. And if there are differences in language or culture, these barriers may loom large, even though no one intended them to do so.

In planning for conferences, remember that students live within many family constellations. Besides the traditional, there are many single-parent families; and grandparents and other relatives are often the caregivers. Students may also live in foster homes or agency-sponsored group homes. It's up to school employees to be sensitive to family and home situations and to make all families and caregivers feel comfortable at their schools.

The question of including students in parent-teacher conferences will have many answers, according to the preferences and habits of individual teachers and schools. However, the advantages of including students are worth the effort. The presence of the student means that all the parties have heard the same conference, the same discussions, and the same recommendations. The student will have heard her parent and teacher come to agreement on major strategies for improvements in conduct or achievement. There is, therefore, little chance for a "he said-she said" argument. Still more important is the effect of gaining the student's opinions and buy-in, so that he fully participates in setting the goals and is therefore able to feel ownership for them. In the final analysis, student achievement requires *the student* to learn personal responsibility within the support offered by home and school;

participating in parent-teacher conferences can serve as an opportunity for taking that responsibility.

It may be helpful to think of the stages in a typical conference, because educators usually possess the social skills needed for each stage. It may also be helpful to imagine the communications skills that are likely to come into play during each stage, as a way of clarifying just what kinds of professional behavior are needed during the entire conference.

## Stage 1: Before the Conference— Preparing the "Lesson Plan"

Before the conference, prepare a "lesson plan" just as you would for a tutoring session with an individual student. Identify the major topics for discussion, including the general overview of the student's performance and conduct, information about the curriculum, and any other pertinent topics. Collect the samples of the student's work that you will present during the conference, and prepare the setting. An informal setting, with chairs side by side at a table, usually puts people at ease, at least more so than when the teacher stays behind the desk and asks the parent to sit on the other side. Make a list of questions or concerns you want to address, and organize any newsletters or announcements prepared for all families for distribution at the time. You'll feel more comfortable and get better results from the conference if your planning is complete.

*Skills:* Planning the session; arranging an informal setting.

## Stage 2: Curtain Up— Forecasting Parental Concerns

Also, before the conference, pretend you're a fortuneteller, and hypothesize what the family's concerns may be. Consider what the student has conveyed about home and family to you and about you to the family. Look for clues about the parent's values, interests, concerns, and so forth. Put yourself in his or her shoes. Recognize that school may be a hostile place to this person, that he or she may feel very shy or very arrogant, or may be anxious, apathetic, or in between. Prepare to maintain a calm, reassuring demeanor when the parent arrives.

*Skills:* Empathizing with another person; reserving judgment; interpreting nonverbal cues and hidden meanings; inferring values from limited evidence; predicting attitude from experiences.

## Stage 3: The Welcome— Playing Host or Hostess

Now pretend you're the host or hostess at a social event. Smile. Try to put the parent at ease. Set the stage for a friendly exchange and an ongoing relationship. And check your earlier forecast: compare the person's actual appearance with your collection of information about him or her. Be open-minded about the new information you are likely to learn.

*Skills:* Empathizing; smiling warmly and sincerely; arranging conference area for easy communications; checking your assessments from Stage 2.

## Stage 4: Getting Started—
## Calling the Meeting to Order

Quickly you become the chairperson of the meeting. It's up to you to get the conference under way with some kind of opening remark. It may be a statement, general or specific, or a question. You may refer to the reason you or the parent requested the conference, and you should inquire about any concerns the parent or student has. Be sure to incorporate these into your "lesson plan" by jotting them down so that the parent can see that you are taking them seriously.

*Skills:* Taking initiative; setting a purpose; expanding the agenda.

## Stage 5: Showing and Telling—
## Teaching the Lesson

Now you're back in the role of teacher. You may share, converse, commiserate, explain, listen, and so on—but the key word is *describe*. You are trying to convey to the parent and the student what the student's work is like. Show the samples of the student's work. Tell about the student's study habits, comments, looks, actions, words, likes, and dislikes. Use simple, direct language—descriptive language without jargon and without blaming or negativity. You may need to make comparisons among subjects or tasks. Be descriptive, not judgmental. Do not criticize or become negative in tone; instead, remain calm, reassuring, and factual. Convey the impression that you have succeeded with many similar situations and that you are likely to succeed with this student, too. Smile.

*Skills:* Using descriptive language; avoiding labels, evaluative terms, and absolutes.

## Stage 6: Getting It Right—
## Leading the Discussion

Take the time to be a discussion leader. You may find it natural to clarify and confirm various points all along; but if you don't, take time to do so at this stage. Find out what the parent or caregiver thinks about the student's work and attitudes. Ask whether your descriptions are making sense to him or her, and ask for stories or anecdotes about the student's behavior at home. Ask for clarification of anything that is unclear, or restate a concern in your own words, and ask whether you've grasped the idea correctly. Determine areas in which you and the parent have similar perceptions and areas in which you do not. You have presented the evidence of the student's performance, you have described the student's behavior and attitudes, and you have arrived at some level of agreement with the parent—where do you go from here?

*Skills:* Paraphrasing; active listening; summarizing; asking for clarification; recognizing differences and likenesses.

## Stage 7: Setting Goals—
## Looking to the Future

Now you're the teacher again. Review the points of agreement, and state your conclusions and recommendations. You may outline options and discuss possible outcomes and examples. As you state (or restate) your recommendations, try to arrive at agreement for your role, the parent's role, and the student's role in carrying out the recommendations. Under no circumstances should you promise benefits that may not materialize. You, the parent, and the student should leave the conference with common understandings about the recommendations. These should represent goals for improvement that all of you support. Writing them down, even in an abbreviated form, is a good idea; or you can develop formal contracts, if that is necessary. Then set the first checkpoint for getting back together, usually by phone in two weeks, to see whether the strategies you've agreed upon are having the desired results. If they aren't working, adjust them or alter them, and try again, setting another checkpoint. The purpose of the checkpoints is to assure the parent that you are serious about improvement efforts and willing to try other approaches to ensure success for the student.

*Skills:* Diagnosing student characteristics; prescribing strategies for improvement (if needed); maintaining communication with the parent and the student; taking the initiative; avoiding use of sales pitches and propaganda.

## Stage 8: Concluding the Conference— Keeping the Relationship Warm and Friendly

You're back to the host or hostess role. It's time for warm thanks, a handshake, a nod, and more smiles. Stand up, if you must, to indicate the end of the conference, especially if you have another conference scheduled immediately. Briefly repeat the date of the first checkpoint, and express your sincere desire to make school a successful experience for the student and the family.

*Skills:* Staying on schedule.

Many situations call for specialized conferences, such as those required for special education students. To adapt this protocol for such purposes, it is necessary to incorporate the legal requirements. Individual schools and teachers can readily adapt these stages to suit local situations and preferences.

## Appendix I

# Media Relations at a Glance

Make friends with the media. Don't call them *the media*—call them by their names. And remember, "They have more ink than you do" (and more film). They also have deadlines, competition for jobs and stories, and families to feed. Always write thank-you notes to them for good—even for fair—stories. Invite them to your building and offer them coffee or lunch—free. They are opinion leaders in the community: Treat them like wonderful human beings.

## Handling the Good News

• Give reporters *advance* notice of events and programs you want to publicize, not after-the-fact notice.

• Think in pictures. How can you make your story appealing on camera?

• Provide just the facts, and keep it short when writing news releases or notices. Remember your grade school lessons about journalism, and tell reporters the *who, what, when, where, how,* and *why* of the story. Remember news releases are the workhorses of the news media; you should be getting them out every week.

• Ask "What's your deadline?" or "When do you need it?" The news business is time

sensitive. Use this fact to your advantage—help reporters manage their time requirements. Then you become one of the good guys/gals in their books. Always get back to them promptly.

• Be persistent; don't give up. If your story doesn't make the news this week, keep trying. You may be lucky next time and pitch a story on a slow news day. Stay in touch with reporters and editors, and keep a "good news" story always ready on your desk.

## Handling the Bad News

• Always tell the truth. Your integrity and credibility are at stake. But do not speculate, and do not be precise when you can't be. In your own mind, be clear about the difference between hearsay and facts. When confidentiality requirements limit what you can say, be straightforward and consistent—just stop talking.

• Always respond to inquiries, even if you are not going on camera or have little to say.

• Prepare your responses ahead of any interview, such as "We estimate between 15 and 20 students got sick . . ." or "The matter is under investigation, and the facts are not in yet . . ." or "I am really not able to answer that question." Be low-key on camera or in the interview. If you are tense, your voice will reveal that, whether you want it to or not.

• Learn to give "your message" rather than just answering a question. This means preparing proactive responses. For example, if you are asked why students should be punished for carrying beepers, say "Well, it's against the law, to begin with . . . but when I was young, I didn't need a beeper to stay in touch with my friends, did you?" Do not restate the question; the question is not your message.

• Do not explain too much. Educators are in the habit of explaining—it's part of teaching. But in the news business, explaining is tricky. For example, if you try to explain "alternative assessments," you are likely to use education jargon that is not clear to the public. If you must explain, use examples people are familiar with. To explain portfolios and exhibitions, you could use examples such as an artist's portfolio as a collection of work over time or a basketball game as an exhibition in which performance is judged, the same as a science fair. Be aware the reporter may not really be interested in the uses of math manipulatives, for example, but may be asking a leading question about whether students are still memorizing math facts, to create controversy. You can respond, "We still teach math facts, don't you worry" or "We still have spelling lessons every day." Your job is to reassure the public, not to convert them to faith in what they may consider fads.

• Do not blame others for a crisis, even if they deserve it.

• Prepare emergency and crisis management procedures for your staff, and write everything down, along with phone numbers and checklists; put the information in a binder so that anyone can take the binder and fill in during a crisis. It's a good idea to note the names of reporter-friends on this list, too, so you or your staff or volunteer can call someone you know and trust.

• Do hold reporters accountable. If their work is inaccurate or biased, write a letter detailing why it is so. If their methods are unethical, say so, in writing. After the first such incident with any one reporter, send a copy of your complaint to the editor or news director. And, if you don't want the letter to appear in print, say it is not for publication.

• Learn to write your own editorials to "set the record straight." Most papers like opposing opinions and perspectives and will welcome your effort. Have a trusted colleague or several read your composition for tone and accuracy before you send it to the paper.

• "This, too, will pass." Remember, even bad news doesn't last long, as a rule. Keep your sense of humor.

• Always debrief a crisis with your staff so you can improve your responses next time.

## Appendix J

# Resources

**A-Plus Communications**
Arlington Courthouse Plaza I
2200 Clarendon Blvd., Suite 1102
Arlington, VA 22201
Phone: (703) 524-7325
Fax: (703) 528-9692
Web site: http://www.ksagroup.com/aplus

A-Plus Communications, spearheaded by Andy Plattner and Adam Kernan-Schloss, consults with educational organizations about marketing and communications.

**Arch Lustberg Communications**
1899 L St., N.W., Suite 1010
Washington, DC 20036
Phone: (202) 833-4343

Arch Lustberg Communications offers *The Lustberg Communicator*, a newsletter especially helpful in preparing for TV coverage. Arch also trains administrators by role-playing on-camera media interviews about local issues.

**Aspen Publishers, Inc.**
200 Orchard Ridge Dr.
Gaithersburg, MD 20878
Phone: (301) 417-7500; Orders: 1-800-638-8437
Fax: (301) 417-7550

Web site: http://www.educationdaily.com/

Aspen Publishers now offers *Education Daily*, a daily newsletter reporting policy developments in Washington, D.C., especially suited for governmental liaison work. Subscriptions are available for e-mail, Web, or print versions of this newsletter. Try 10 days free of the e-mail version.

**Association for Supervision and Curriculum Development (ASCD)**
1703 N. Beauregard St.
Alexandria, VA 22311-1714
Phone: (703) 578-9600 or 1-800-933-2723, then press 2
Fax: (703) 575-5400
E-mail: info@ascd.org
Web site: http://www.ascd.org

ASCD offers a video training package, *Building Support for Public Education*, which features two videotapes. *Communicating and Working with the Public* describes a comprehensive communications program in a large public school system; *Providing Options to Meet Diverse Needs* outlines community outreach in a smaller district where religious issues threatened to disrupt public support. The package includes an excellent facilitator's manual for use with the tapes. Price is $395.

Also available from ASCD:

• *Quick Response: A Step-by-Step Guide to Crisis Management for Principals, Counselors, and Teachers*, a binder giving procedures for 15 different crisis situations, with tabbed sections and pull-out folders for use by key staff members. Developed in 1997 by Educational Service District 105, Yakima, Washington. Member price is $185.

• *Quick Reference: Seven Important Steps to Take in a Crisis*, a flipbook composed of an easy-to-follow checklist to use during a crisis, with spaces for local phone numbers. Developed in 1997 by Educational Service District 105, Yakima, Washington. Member price is $17.95.

• *Involving Parents in Education*, a video program that shows scenes from schools with successful parent involvement programs. The video can help educators improve parents' attitudes toward schooling, build a natural bridge between school and home, and help parents work with their children on homework. Developed in 1992 by ASCD. One 30-minute videotape with a 54-page Leader's Guide. Member price is $290.

• *How to Create Successful Parent-Student Conferences*, a video that helps teachers plan and conduct productive conferences that build rapport and create a winning situation for students, parents, guardians, and teachers. Developed in 1998 by ASCD. Approximately 15 minutes. Member price is $79.

*A Citizen's Guide on Using the Freedom of Information Act and the Privacy Act of 1974 to Request Government Records.* A clearly written overview of the provisions of these two federal laws, this small, very useful booklet is available from the U.S. Government Printing Office (GPO) for $5.00. Phone the GPO Order Desk between 7:30 a.m. and 5:30 p.m., eastern time, Monday through Friday, at 202-512-1800, or fax order to 202-512-2250. You may also go to the GPO Web site and find the Sales Product Catalog (http://www.gpo.gov).

*Early Warning, Timely Response: A Guide to Safe Schools.* This 36-page booklet offers practical perspectives and helpful suggestions regarding school climate, early warning signs, interventions for troubled children, and responding to crises. Review the text of the booklet at the U.S. Department of Education Web site (http://www.ed.gov/offices/OSERS/OSEP/earlywrn.html) or call 1-877-4ED-PUBS to request a copy.

**EdPress—The Association of Educational Publishers**
Rowan University
201 Mullica Hill Rd.
Glassboro, NJ 08028-1701
Phone: (609) 256-4610
Fax: (609) 256-4926
E-mail: EdPress@aol.com
Web site: http://www.edpress.org

EdPress is an independent professional organization for publishers, editors, and others involved in educational publishing. For schools and school systems, EdPress offers the Annual Distinguished Achievement Awards programs in educational publishing and educational technology. These awards recognize excellence throughout the country, and the EdPress seal signifies quality to readers and viewers.

### Education Commission of the States (ECS)

ECS Distribution Center
707 17th St., Suite 2700
Denver, CO 80202-3427
Phone: (303) 299-3692
Web site: http://www.ecs.org

Education Commission of the States (ECS), with A-Plus Communications, offers *Building Community Support for Schools: A Practical Guide to Strategic Communications*, by Arleen Arnsparger, Adam Kernan-Schloss, Andy Plattner, and Sylvia Soholt. This 28-page softcover book is available from ECS for $10.00 plus postage and handling. It's clearly written, concise, well organized, and full of practical ideas.

ECS also offers *Do-It-Yourself Focus Groups: A Low Cost Way to Listen to Your Community*, by Arleen Arnsparger and Marjorie A. Ledell. This 25-page guide is available for $10.00 plus postage and handling. Describing the uses of focus groups for determining public opinion, this guide provides assistance for the facilitator's role, reporting strategies, sample response forms, logistical helps, and much more.

### FamilyEducation Company

20 Park Plaza, Suite 1215
Boston, MA 02116
Phone: 1-800-927-6006, ext. 1684
Fax: (617) 542-6564
Web site: http://familyeducation.com
E-mail: community@familyeducation.com

The FamilyEducation Company, a partner of ASCD, offers FREE assistance to schools in creating and maintaining school and district Web sites, through the FamilyEducation Network (FEN). FEN provides a low-maintenance solution for establishing or enhancing a Web presence, including FEN InterCom Web Tools and tech support. Districts and schools provide a "system director" for local maintenance; FEN offers criteria for the qualifications of that person and others who may serve on the Web site team. According to Dave Leonard, Manager of Education Partnerships, "We provide school districts with a 'parent involvement' Web site that links parents to not only their child's school, but also to thousands of pages of parenting and education information, experts, state and national resources, and discussions with other parents nationwide."

### Bernard C. Harris Publishing Company, Inc.

3 Barker Ave.
White Plains, NY 10601
Phone: 1-800-326-6600
Fax: (914) 287-2244
Web site: http://www.bcharrispub.com

Harris Publishing can provide the information you need to reach your alumni, start or enhance an alumni association or foundation, and build community support. They research current residential and professional information on alumni, compile the information, and produce alumni directories for public high schools, at no cost to the institution, through their Graduate Connection Program. The school receives an updated alumni database on Harris's exclusive database management software, also at no cost.

The following booklets are available free from Harris Publishing:

- *How to Start an Alumni Association*
- *How to Start a Foundation*
- *Creative Ways to Raise Funds and Cultivate Alumni*

## Illinois Association of School Boards (IASB)

School Public Relations Service
430 E. Vine St.
Springfield, IL 62703-2236
Phone: (217) 528-9688

IASB offers a subscription service providing newsletters for parents and opinion leaders, as well as seasonal clip art. Available for $40 annually, print materials only; or $60 annually, print materials plus diskette.

## International Alliance for Invitational Education

c/o Curry Building, School of Education
The University of North Carolina at Greensboro
Greensboro, NC 27412-5001
Phone: (336) 334-3431
Fax: (336) 334-3433
Web site: http://www.uncg.edu/ced/iaie

The International Alliance for Invitational Education offers membership in this international network of 1,200 professionals in education and other helping professions for $25 annually. The Alliance supports a fresh and innovative approach to academic learning, interpersonal relationships, emotional climate, human motivation, and the educative process. Codirected by Betty L. Siegel and William W. Purkey, the Alliance sponsors an annual awards program to recognize Inviting Schools, Inviting Colleges, and Inviting School Districts.

## Ketchum Public Relations

For a definitive treatment of public relations research, consult *A Guide to Public Relations Research* by Walter K. Lindenmann of Ketchum Public Relations Worldwide. For more information, call (212) 448-4200 or (212) 448-4213. This resource is intended for practitioners; it offers many additional resources, organizations, a glossary, and guidelines.

## National Association of Partners in Education (NAPE)

901 N. Pitt St., Suite 320
Alexandria, VA 22314
Phone: (703) 836-4880
Fax: (703) 836-6941
Web site: http://www.napehq.org

The National Association of Partners in Education (NAPE) is an international network of partnership professionals, with 7,500 members and 34 state affiliates. NAPE offers membership, publications, and additional resources for beginning or revitalizing a business-education partnership.

**National Educational Service (NES)**
1252 Loesch Rd.
P.O. Box 8
Bloomington, IN 47402
Phone: 1-800-733-6786 or (812) 336-7700
Web site: http://www.nes.org

National Educational Service offers *How Smart Schools Get and Keep Community Support*, published in 1994, for $19.95, with bulk discounts available. This book provides detailed assistance for assessing public opinion, including surveys, focus groups, and demographic studies, as well as general guidance for communications. Also available is *Parents Assuring Student Success*, by John Ban, for $21.95, a step-by-step parent involvement program for grades K–12, addressing student achievement through such topics as test preparation, using time wisely, and developing positive attitudes. A good source for helping teachers reach out to parents is a two-program video series, *Partners Toward Achievement*, with Hillery Motsinger, for $139.

**National Parent-Teacher Association (PTA)**
330 N. Wabash Ave., Suite 2100
Chicago, IL 60611-3690
Phone: (312) 670-6782
Web site: http://www.pta.org/

The PTA is the oldest and largest volunteer association in the United States working exclusively on behalf of children and youth, with more than 6.5 million members and 26,000 local units. Of special interest is a publication, *National Standards for Parent/Family Involvement Programs*, which offers guidelines

for establishing and maintaining such programs.

**National School Public Relations Association (NSPRA)**
15948 Derwood Rd.
Rockville, MD 20855
Phone: (301) 519-0496
Fax: (301) 519-0494
Web site: http://www.nspra.org

NSPRA offers a variety of publications, all excellent, as well as communications audits, workshops, and conferences. Their resources include the following:

• *The Complete Crisis Communications Management Manual for Schools*, one of the best available. Includes action steps for dealing with major crises, do's and don'ts for working with the media, and checklists for school employees on dealing with hazards. Price: $139 plus shipping and handling; for $50 additional, includes disk so you can customize the contents.

• *Practical PR for Principals*, a binder filled with ready-to-use resources including more than 100 easy-to-use PR ideas, advice for communicating with parents, and strategies for turning your staff into PR ambassadors. Price: $89 for orders of 1–10, plus shipping and handling.

• *The ABC Complete Book of School Marketing*, written by Bill Banach, including practical advice, tactics, examples, and forms to get your marketing program rolling. Price: $75 plus shipping and handling.

• *Win at the Polls*, newly revised 300-page handbook for passing your next bond issue or school finance campaign. Includes community research methods, precinct analysis, and samples of winning materials from successful campaigns. Price: $195 plus shipping and handling.

• *Making and Marketing Your School the School of Choice,* a 100-page handbook including research on why parents choose a school, techniques for becoming a customer-friendly school, and steps to take in marketing your school in your community. Price: $39.95 plus shipping and handling.

• *School Communication Workshop Kit,* the entire package needed for developing a communications program geared to your situation, including the identification of internal and external publics, development of a feedback process, and evaluation methods. Price: $95 plus shipping and handling.

• Also available from NSPRA: Speaker Service, which offers a roster of experienced keynoters and workshop leaders on school communications, including Joseph Lowenthal, past president of NSPRA, who has in-depth experience in working with media liaisons, as well as a host of other areas. For more information, call Rich Bagin, executive director of NSPRA, at (301) 519-0496.

### National School Safety Center (NSSC)
141 Duesenberg Drive, Suite 11
Westlake Village, CA 91362
Phone: (805) 373-9977
Fax: (805) 373-9277
Web site: http://www.nssc1.org

NSSC offers *Educated Public Relations: School Safety 101,* a 64-page softcover book by Stuart Greenbaum, Blanca Gonzalez, and Nancy Ackley. This book provides "101 school safety ideas" that reflect broad public engagement strategies, along with a list of resources. Also available are many publications on school safety.

### National Study of School Evaluation (NSSE)
1699 E. Woodfield Rd., Suite 406
Schaumburg, IL 60173
Phone: 1-800-THE-NSSE
Web site: http://www.nsse.org

The National Study of School Evaluation offers Opinion Inventories for Students, Teachers, Parents and Community Members; sample packets are available for $10.00 plus $5.00 shipping charges. These inventories address issues of special concern to each constituent group and may also be customized by the addition of as many as 20 questions based on local concerns. The Administrator's Manual contains advice about conducting the surveys, technical information about sampling procedures, and sample cover letters. NSSE can also provide scoring and analysis services and assistance with executive summary presentation reports.

### Phi Delta Kappa International
408 N. Union
P.O. Box 789
Bloomington, IN 47404-0789
Phone: (812) 339-1156 or 1-800-766-1156
Fax: (812) 339-0018
E-mail: headquarters@pdkintl.org
Web site: http://www.pdkintl.org

*Phi Delta Kappa Washington Newsletter*, published quarterly for members, is an excellent source of policy developments focused on Washington, D.C., valuable for governmental liaison work.

### Public Agenda

6 E. 39th St., 9th Floor
New York, NY 10016
Phone: (212) 686-6610
Fax: (212) 889-3461
Web site: http://www.publicagenda.org

Public Agenda assesses public opinion on timely education issues and offers practical strategies for public engagement. Publications of special interest are *Getting By: What American Teenagers Really Think About Their Schools* ($10.00), *Assignment Incomplete: The Unfinished Business of Education Reform* ($10.00), and *First Things First: What Americans Expect from Public Schools* ($10.00). Public Agenda has documented the disconnect between education reformers and public opinion and is therefore of particular importance in building public support for schools.

### Ragan Communications, Inc.

316 N. Michigan Avenue, Suite 300
Chicago, IL 60601
Phone: 1-800-878-5331
Web site: http://www.ragan.com

Ragan attracts corporate PR pros, plus some from the nonprofit sector. Ragan offers regional workshops and excellent publications, such as *Media Relations Tactics*, by Ed Bauer, a 61-page

handbook summarizing the full contingent of how-to-do-it ideas. Also useful is *Do-It-Yourself Public Relations*, a 35-page collection of tips and techniques, in a well-organized and easy-to-follow format, also by Ed Bauer. Call for a publications list to see all their offerings.

### Sage Publications

2455 Teller Rd.
Thousand Oaks, CA 91320-2218
Phone: (805) 499-9774
E-mail: order@sagepub.com
Web site: http://www.sagepub.com

Sage Publications offers six volumes providing in-depth treatment of focus group research. The titles are *The Focus Group Guidebook*, *Planning Focus Groups*, *Developing Questions for Focus Groups*, *Moderating Focus Groups*, *Involving Community Members in Focus Groups*, and *Analyzing and Reporting Focus Group Results*. The authors are David L. Morgan of Portland State University and Richard A. Krueger and Jean A. King of the University of Minnesota. These materials are excellent, providing a serious research orientation.

### Wadsworth Publishing Company

10 Davis Dr.
Belmont, CA 94002
Web site: http://www.wadsworth.com/
    home.html

Wadsworth offers *Electronic Public Relations*, a 218-page softcover book including an overview of public relations history, current and emerging technologies, the varied audiences for electronic communications, and the future of electronic public relations. It includes many examples from the corporate sector and from nonprofits. Written by Eugene Marlow and Janice Sileo.

# Glossary

**audience impressions**—an estimate of the number of people reached by publications or media outlets

**bad ink**—coverage in the news media with a negative outcome or image

**baseline communications**—aspect of a comprehensive communications program designed to meet basic, ongoing information needs in the community

**clip art**—readymade motifs, icons, illustrations, and other types of artwork, available electronically or in print

**communications**—a general term referring to comprehensive efforts to promote products and services, enhance the image of an organization, and provide information about an organization

**community relations**—a program of outreach from the school system to the community, coordinated to maintain connections with constituents; may include communications

**copy house**—a business specializing in copy services and other preparation and duplication services, especially for multiple copies

**crisis communications**—the part of a comprehensive communications program dealing with emergency situations

**early warning system**—a planned strategy for notifying the superintendent or other central office staffers about a crisis or emergency in a school

**editing suite**—a facility offering the technical equipment and capacity for editing videos

**embargo**—a request to reporters and editors to refrain from printing or broadcasting a news item until an appropriate time

**focus group**—(1) a group of people representing the audience intended for a particular publication, video, home page, or Web site or (2) a group convened to identify emerging issues and to give opinions about hot topics

**Freedom of Information Act**—federal and state laws ensuring the access of citizens to government records or information and requiring government entities to provide copies of the records or information, except for certain exemptions

**good ink**—coverage in the news media with a positive slant or image; the desirable results of a communications program

**hard news**—traditional news stories (not feature stories or human interest pieces), usually about such topics as school board actions, budgets, boundary or attendance zones, curriculum controversies, personnel issues, student test scores, scandals, arrests, and the like

**home page**—a Web site accessed through the Internet, usually providing links to information about the person or organization originating it

**image enhancement**—efforts to show an organization at its best; a public relations campaign directed at the goal of improving public or client perceptions of an organization

**Intranet**—a local private network (as opposed to the public Internet) connecting the offices or facilities of an organization for purposes of internal communications only

**issue management** or **issues management**—the process of identifying current and emerging opinions, impressions, and responses from customers, audiences, or community that have the potential of becoming major issues for the organization to address

**mail house**—a business specializing in assisting organizations or persons in preparing multiple copies of publications for mailing

**marketing**—a concerted effort or communications campaign to sell products or services, convey the benefits of membership in an organization, or publicize the services or benefits provided by an organization

**news hook**—a means of engaging or "hooking" attention, such as the most exciting item selected as the lead in a news release; the major point selected for pitching a story

**pitch**—to promote actively and vigorously any particular story or news item with reporters and editors

**public engagement**—actual participation by the public in public affairs, including education; referring to strategies that go beyond providing public information or ensuring good public relations to promoting substantive, participatory roles for citizens in governance matters

**public information**—the provision of information about an organization; information required by the public's right to know; or information required to be provided by the Freedom of Information Act

**public relations**—the promotions and community outreach designed to enhance the image and promote the presence of an organization in its community or arena

**publicity**—old grassroots club word denoting the promotion of news about one's club or organization

**soft news**—the human side of the news: awards, instructional programs, volunteer recognitions, student achievements, personal insights into teachers' lives, and so forth

**spin**—slant, perspective, or a technique of persuasion involving selecting the information to present, the information to emphasize, and the information to omit, especially that deemed nonessential or negative to the person or organization at the center of the news

**URL**—universal resource locator; the designation for a Web site or home page on the Internet

# Index

---

Note: Illustrations are indicated by (fig) following the page number.

# About the Author

**A**nne Meek is an education consultant living in Norfolk, Virginia. She has served as an early childhood teacher, a middle school teacher, and a principal. After several years as managing editor of *Educational Leadership* for ASCD, she led communications efforts for a large city school system, the Virginia Beach City (Virginia) Public Schools, creating print and video materials for external and internal audiences, working with the media, and providing executive services to the superintendent and school board.

Meek is the editor of the book *Designing Places for Learning,* published by ASCD in 1995; coeditor of *Children, Learning, and School Design,* a collection of papers from the First National Invitational Conference for Architects and Educators; and has written numerous articles for magazines, professional journals, and newsletters.

Anne Meek
1930 Hunters Trail
Norfolk, VA 23518
Phone: (757) 857-3802
E-mail: annemeek@aol.com